2,024 QI FACTS

John Lloyd CBE is the creator of QI and the host of
BBC Radio 4's *The Museum of Curiosity*. He was
the original producer of *The News Quiz, To the
Manor Born, Not the Nine O'Clock News,
Spitting Image* and *Blackadder*.
His favourite page is 492.

James Harkin, QI's Head of Research, is
known as 'Turbo' for his phenomenal work rate.
He is one of the presenters of the hit podcast
No Such Thing As A Fish, which sold out the
Sydney Opera House on tour in 2018.
His favourite page is 271.

Anne Miller is a senior researcher and writer
for QI. In 2017, she became an assistant producer
of BBC2's *QI*, and is also co-producer of
Radio 4's *The Museum of Curiosity*.
Her favourite page is 144.

*For more from the team behind QI, visit qi.com.
You can also follow QI's fact-filled Twitter account
@qikipedia and listen to the researchers' weekly
podcast at nosuchthingasafish.com*

A QUITE INTERESTING BOOK

2,024 QI FACTS

TO STOP YOU IN YOUR TRACKS

Compiled by
John Lloyd, James Harkin
& Anne Miller

NUMBER SEVEN IN THE QI FACTS SERIES

FABER & FABER

First published in 2018
by Faber & Faber Ltd
Bloomsbury House
74–77 Great Russell Street
London WC1B 3DA

Typeset by Ian Bahrami
Printed and bound in England by CPI Group (UK) Ltd,
Croydon CR0 4YY

The right of QI Ltd to be identified as author of this work
has been asserted in accordance with Section 77 of
the Copyright, Designs and Patents Act 1988

A CIP record for this book
is available from the British Library

ISBN 978–0–571–34896–1

FSC
www.fsc.org
MIX
Paper from
responsible sources
FSC® C020471

6 8 10 9 7

Contents

[v]

The last thing one knows when writing
a book is what to put first.

BLAISE PASCAL

(1623–62)

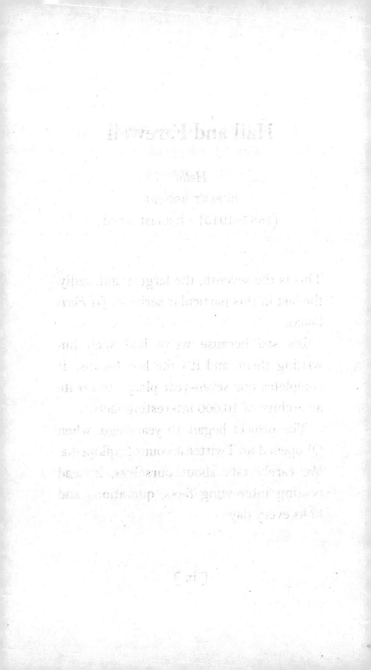

Hail and Farewell

Hello.

RUPERT BROOKE

(1887–1915) – his last word

This is the seventh, the largest and, sadly, the last in this particular series of *QI Facts* books.

It's sad because we've had such fun writing them, and it's the last because it completes our seven-year plan – to create an archive of 10,000 interesting facts.

The project began 10 years ago, when QI opened its Twitter account @qikipedia. We rarely talk about ourselves, instead posting interesting facts, quotations and links every day.

When we started, we did it just for fun, and it quickly proved absurdly addictive. One of the most interesting (and entirely unexpected) side effects of working at QI is that no one takes ownership of the information they unearth. When we find anything out, our first instinct is to share it – you just *have* to tell someone. And nowadays, we share what we discover with almost a million followers.

Quite Interesting Ltd – the company behind QI, and the one we all work for – is a tiny outfit, with barely a dozen permanent staff, and this joy of finding out and sharing is at the heart of everything we do. Our TV show, BBC2's *QI* itself, our Radio 4 show *The Museum of Curiosity*, our podcast *No Such Thing As A Fish* and our pocket-sized library of QI books are all driven by it.

To get you up in the morning, nothing beats looking forward to an interesting day. In the words of Johann Wolfgang von Goethe (1749–1832), 'Thinking is more interesting than knowing, but less interesting than looking.' High-minded though this may sound, during its early years @qikipedia came under pressure from QI's senior management (or Sarah, as we know her). What was the point of it (apart from the undoubted larks, that is)? At first, she was sort of pacified with the words 'brand-building exercise', but then we came up with the neat idea that it could be used for staff training.

And indeed, every new QI researcher since has started out on Twitter. Especially in the days when tweets were limited to 140 characters, it taught concision, good writing and, because the audience is so opinionated, the vital importance of accuracy. Most of all, you learn extremely fast what is and what is not interesting. On Twitter, if you're not famous, you'd better be interesting or funny, or no one will show up.

After three years of steady posting, it eventually occurred to one of us – no one can remember who – that this daily stream of beguiling nuggets could form the basis of a book. (We use all sorts of other sources of course, but this crisp expression of information arose out of our Twitter style.) And so, *1,227 QI Facts to Blow Your Socks Off* was born.

This was followed by *1,339 QI Facts to Make Your Jaw Drop*, *1,411 QI Facts to Knock You Sideways*, *1,234 QI Facts to Leave You Speechless*, *1,342 QI Facts to Leave You Flabbergasted*, *1,423 QI Facts to Bowl You*

Over – and now this one, *2,024 QI Facts to Stop You in Your Tracks.*

Add them all together and it comes to a nice round 10,000 facts.

In ancient Chinese philosophy, the number 10,000 is used to mean 'the infinite multiplicity of all forms and beings in existence'. While we certainly don't think we've got that far, we believe we can reasonably stake a claim to having assembled the largest collection of interesting one-line facts in the history of the human race.

If you learn each one off by heart, having also read all the background information that can be found by using the Operating Instructions that follow, there is a 99.99% chance that you will become the best-educated and most interesting person you know.

Yes, you too can appear to be a genius in just three months, for less than the price of a taxi ride from Piccadilly Circus to Heathrow airport.

Start by reading this book, and have fun.

Or hail away.

You decide.

JOHN LLOYD, JAMES HARKIN
& ANNE MILLER

Operating Instructions

Never check an interesting fact.

HOWARD HUGHES

(1905–76)

In his day, Howard Hughes was one of the richest people in the world, so his advice is not to be sniffed at. If you agree with him, there's no need to read on.

Most of the facts in this book are surprising, and a fair few are scarcely credible. If you doubt anything you see, here's what to do. Go online to:

qi.com/2024

In the search box, enter the page number of the fact you want to check. This will reveal our source for each piece of information on the page, like this:

| Page in book | Page in source finder |

Click on the appropriate link to get all the background details on the fact.

You can read the whole of this book in a couple of hours, but the extra reading provided by the source finder should keep you busy for weeks.

This is not just a big book; it's also a little window opening onto the universe.

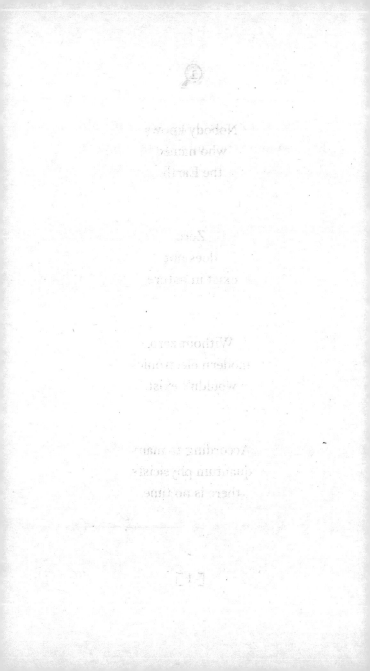

Nobody knows
who named
the Earth.

Zero
does not
exist in nature.

Without zero,
modern electronics
wouldn't exist.

According to many
quantum physicists,
there is no time.

'Time'
is the most
used noun in
the English language.

The present moment
is the most disorganised
the universe has
ever been.

People who have had their
frown lines removed with Botox
find it harder to read
difficult sentences.

An altered state
of consciousness can
be achieved by staring
into someone's eyes
for 10 minutes.

According to its CEO,
Apple, Inc. is a
conscious
being.

A glass
of Calvados
contains seven
apples.

There is
enough room in
the human memory
for 300 years of
television.

Loganamnosis
is an obsessive searching
for a forgotten word.

The word for
'the inside of the elbow'
is *chelidon*.

People who don't
have a tissue should
sneeze into their chelidon,
not their hand.

A handshake
begins and ends
every game of
curling.

In Sweden,
millennials are called
'the Curling Generation',
because all obstacles have
been brushed from their
path by their parents.

All Olympic
curling stones come
from one uninhabited
island 10 miles
from Glasgow.

In 2017,
Glasgow was voted
the most dangerous and
also the friendliest city
in Scotland.

Eyebrows evolved to
make humans look friendly
to one another.

In the 10 seasons of *Friends*,
the six main characters
drink 1,154 cups
of coffee.

The Hitler Youth
only drank decaf
coffee.

Rats with
low social status
drink more than those
with high social status.

20,112 rats were
caught and killed in Hanoi
on a single day in 1902.

On a single day in 2018,
volunteers in India planted
66 million trees.

The palm trees
in Los Angeles are the
result of a job-creation scheme
in the 1930s.

The way tree tops
avoid touching each other
as they grow is called
'crown shyness'.

The Queen
practises wearing her crown
for a week before the
Queen's Speech.

The Queen takes a
monogrammed kettle
with her on all
foreign trips.

The Teabag Boys,
Yak Balls, Cecil Otter and
Bus Driver are all names of
professional rappers.

Every year,
Britons use enough
wrapping paper to
wrap the Moon.

If all the plastic
in the world were
cling film, it could
wrap the Earth.

There is enough
plastic in the world to make
25,000 Empire State Buildings,
80 million blue whales or
a billion elephants.

The Queen has
banned plastic straws
from the royal estates.

The first bendy straws
were designed for
use in hospitals.

The A&E department at
Leicester Royal Infirmary
treated twice as many patients
the weekend Leicester City
won the Premier League.

Football was
banned in London
in 1314 for being
too noisy.

In Arab countries,
poetry competitions
get better TV ratings
than football matches.

Footballers at Sweden's
Östersunds Fotbollsklubb are
contractually obliged to
read Dostoevsky.

France
has short-story
vending machines.

In 2017,
a book called
Forty Minutes Late was
returned to a San Francisco library
100 years late.

More than half of
all meetings
start late.

The chances of surviving
a heart attack increase when the
top doctors are absent from the
hospital attending important
cardiology meetings.

The first meeting of
the War Propaganda Bureau was
attended by Sir Arthur Conan Doyle,
Thomas Hardy, Rudyard Kipling
and H. G. Wells.

The 'coffee break'
was invented in 1952 by
the American Coffee Bureau.

'Bacon and eggs'
was invented by
Sigmund Freud's
nephew.

The Queen
won't reveal
her favourite meal
in case she never gets
served anything else.

For the Queen's Diamond Jubilee,
Marmite brought out a
special edition called
Ma'amite.

Alfred the Butler
is the name of 12 different people
in the Domesday Book.

The bookshelf
was invented by
Christopher Columbus's son.

Children perform
boring tasks better
when dressed
as Batman.

Wonder Woman
was created by the inventor
of the lie detector.

Vranyo is
Russian for lying
even when everyone knows
that's what you're doing.

Mencolek is
Indonesian for
tapping someone on the
opposite shoulder to fool them.

Bamboo sharks
shrug their shoulders
to swallow their food.

In the 1930s,
artist Dorothy Beck invented
an inverted underwater periscope
so she could stay dry while
sketching fish.

Swordfish
track fast-moving prey
in deep, cold water
by heating up
their eyes.

After Apollo 11 landed,
the Moon's temperature
rose by 2°C.

NASA's 'clean rooms' are
infested by microbes that resist
heat, desiccation and radiation
and eat the cleaning products.

The thermostat knobs in many
hotel bedrooms don't work:
they're rigged to save
electricity.

80% of the
'Close Door' buttons
in lifts are just for show:
the doors are
on a timer.

In 1986,
12 jurors got stuck
in an Otis elevator in a
courthouse on their way to
hear a lawsuit against
the Otis Elevator
Company.

In 2017,
a court in Indonesia
blamed an increase in the divorce rate
on the sudden popularity
of pigeon racing.

In Regina, California,
it's illegal to own more
than 90 pigeons.

It's illegal to swim in
the River Seine in Paris.

In professional swimming,
it's against the rules to wear
two swimming costumes.

In public pools
in New York City,
you're not allowed
to hold your breath.

In 2017,
70 students in Maryland
drank so much alcohol at a party
that the air in the house registered
positive on a breathalyser.

'Breeching parties'
celebrated boys getting
their first pair
of trousers.

New Year's Day is
the official birthday of
everyone in Bhutan.

In Johannesburg
on New Year's Day,
it's traditional to throw
an item of furniture
out of a window.

When New Year
was moved in 1751 from
25 March to 1 January,
there were only 282
days in the year.

In ancient Egypt,
the New Year began
whenever the Nile
started to flood.

Ancient Egyptians
mummified their cats and
gave them mummified mice
to torment in the afterlife.

Catalan authorities
regularly check websites
ending with '.cat' to ensure
they're about Catalonia,
not cats.

Savannah
is a breed of cat that
can be trained to play fetch
and go for walks on a lead.

If human eyes were
in the same proportion
as cats' eyes, they'd be
eight inches across.

Honesty boxes
with photos of eyes
stuck on the wall next to them
produce more money.

Painting eyes
on cows' bottoms
stops lions attacking them.

Rabbits hate being
picked up because
they think they're
about to be eaten.

Listening
to talk radio
can put pumas
off their food.

King George VI's wedding
was not broadcast on the radio
in case people listened without
removing their hats.

A radio station in Texas that
burned Beatles records in 1966
was struck by lightning
the next day.

Not realising his
microphone was switched on,
Ronald Reagan once joked
that the US was about
to bomb Russia.

There are
an estimated
14,485 nuclear weapons
in the world today.

Airbnb's HQ
features a replica
of the War Room from
Dr Strangelove.

A supersonic flypast
at Ottawa's new airport in 1959
smashed all the glass in the buildings
and delayed the opening for a year.

The first loop-the-loop roller coaster
had to close down because
so many people were
passing out.

Disneyland
shut down its gondola rides
because too many people were
having sex on them.

When two prime numbers
differ by 6 (e.g. 5 and 11),
they are known as
'sexy primes'.

$$(6 \times 9) + (6 + 9) = 69$$

The Babylonians
were doing trigonometry
3,700 years ago.

5,000 years ago,
humans practised
brain surgery
on cows.

Gaspare Tagliacozzi,
the pioneer of the nose job,
developed his skills at a clinic called
the Hospital of Death.

The surgeon at the
Battle of the Sierra Negra (1794)
averaged one amputation
every four minutes.

Plastic surgeons are
eight times more likely
to have had plastic surgery
than the rest of us.

People who drink
seven cups of coffee a day are
more likely to think they
sense the presence
of dead people.

Poltergeist
is German for
'noisy ghost'.

The first planet discovered
outside the Solar System
was named Poltergeist.

Pluto's moon,
Charon, was named
by its discoverer
after his wife
Char(lene).

Names of
Greek ocean gods
included Poseidon,
Triton, Oceanus
and Doris.

In 2006,
a Greek court
ruled it was no longer
illegal to worship
Greek gods.

The world's
first Christian nation
was Armenia.

Britain's first
vegetarian church
opened in a building called
Beefsteak Chapel.

Avocados
are not vegan.

Mentioning guacamole
on your dating profile gets you
144% more responses.

The first contraceptive pill
was developed from
Mexican yams.

Viagra
can make your urine
turn blue.

Prussian blue
was discovered by a
German chemist trying
to make red.

Red placebo pills
work better
than blue
ones.

Yellow tennis balls,
which look better on colour TV,
were the idea of David Attenborough
when he was Controller of BBC2.

Different tennis balls are used
for men's and women's matches;
the men's are fluffier to
slow them down.

Table tennis
was the first sport to
abolish the distinction between
amateurs and professionals.

Football World Cup referees
have to learn swear words
in other languages.

TITSUP is
a military acronym for
Total Inability To Support
Usual Performance.

SWIPERS is
a retail-industry acronym for
Seemingly Well-Intentioned Patrons
Engaging in Routine Shoplifting.

TASER is
an acronym for
Thomas A. Swift's Electric Rifle.

In 2016,
Australian police
offered cash prizes to
any drivers they found
to be sober.

The oldest known boomerang
is from Poland.

Mount Kosciuszko,
the highest mountain in Australia,
is named after an artificial
mound in Poland.

The summit of
Mount Everest was
once part of the
ocean floor.

The highest mountain
on British soil is
in Antarctica.

At Two Ocean Pass, Wyoming,
a mountain stream splits into two:
one flows into the Atlantic,
the other into the Pacific.

In 1949,
Mole Hill,
West Virginia,
was renamed
Mountain.

Joan Crawford
was named by the readers
of a movie magazine.

On the set of *Jaws*,
the shark was nicknamed Bruce,
after Steven Spielberg's lawyer.

The first crime prosecuted
using fingerprint evidence
was the theft of some
billiard balls.

The largest theft ever investigated
by Quebec police was of
maple syrup.

Between 1935 and 1937,
Wisconsin law required all
restaurant meals to be served
with free cheese.

The first use
of the word 'mammoth'
as an adjective meaning 'big'
referred to a large cheese.

The world's largest asbestos mine
is in Asbest, Russia.

The world's largest paper plane
had a 60-foot wingspan.

Each pod on the
world's largest Ferris wheel is
equipped with a TV screen
to stave off boredom.

Season 7
of *Game of Thrones*
was pirated more than
a billion times.

Michael Bond,
creator of Paddington Bear,
was a camera operator
on *Blue Peter.*

Paddington Bear wears
a hat when swimming because
Michael Bond's father always did,
in case he needed to
raise it politely.

The etiquette experts Debrett's
run classes for five-year-olds
on learning how to navigate
dinner parties.

Alumnesia
is the failure to remember
the name of a former classmate.

Scurryfunge
is to tidy up quickly before
visitors arrive.

Cacozelia
is the use of foreign words
to make one appear
un peu plus cultivé.

Treppenwitz
is German for the witty riposte
that occurs to you
too late.

'Joke' comes
from the same Latin word
as 'jewel'.

The redder a ruby,
the more it costs.

Donald Trump's daughter Tiffany
was named after the
jewellers.

Peter Carl Fabergé
made 50 exquisite Fabergé eggs
and one Fabergé potato.

Until they hatch,
the eggs of cardinal fish
are stored in the males' mouths,
where 30% of them are
regrettably swallowed.

The hands of a human foetus
touching the walls of the womb
causes the fingerprints to form.

Elephant's ear plants
look like they're diseased
so eggs won't be
laid on them.

Elephants
can hear better
with one foot off
the ground.

When his sound system failed,
mime artist Marcel Marceau
cancelled the performance.

The mayor of Bogotá
hired 420 mime artists
to shame traffic violators
into driving better.

The aim of the
sacred combat of the
Moche people of ancient Peru
was to knock your opponent's hat off.

Peruvians are
the world's fastest
workers.

The Latin for 'proud'
is *superbum*.

'Bum'
was defined in
Dr Johnson's *Dictionary*
as 'the part on which we sit'.

The word 'kleptomania'
was coined in the 1860s because
words like 'robbery', 'theft' and 'larceny'
were considered inappropriate
for the upper classes.

A *clank-napper* was
an 18th-century thief who
specialised in stealing
silverware.

The oldest object in
the British crown jewels
is a spoon.

Knife marks on
the oldest known book
of English poetry suggest
it was once used as a
chopping board.

The world's
oldest pot plant
is 243 years old and
weighs one tonne.

The two
oldest men
living in Britain
in 2018 were born
on the same day in 1908.

Blowing out the candles
on a birthday cake increases
the number of bacteria on it
by up to 1,400%.

The least hygienic parts
of an aeroplane are
the tray tables.

Terrifying flights were
prescribed in the 1920s
to cure deafness.

In 1981,
Margaret Thatcher
refused to share Concorde
with a giant panda.

A mother panda
is 800 times larger
than her newborn.

The man who
named the panda
was the younger brother of
the man who named
the pterodactyl.

Sichuanese people who
swallowed needles by mistake
would try to melt them by
drinking panda urine.

The ancient Greeks
cured hangovers by
wrapping their heads
in cabbage leaves.

The man who
coined the term 'nostalgia'
thought it could be cured
by taking laxatives.

Latex
is Latin for
'liquid'.

British Army soldiers
are given anti-bacterial
underpants.

The US military
spends $42 million a year
on Viagra.

The citizens of
the Czech Republic
are the baldest people
in the world.

In Japan,
people with
thin, black, careful
combovers are called
'bar code men'.

At Joan of Arc's trial,
she was asked to comment on
the hairstyles of the saints who
appeared in her visions.

A tiger's
night vision
is six times better
than a human's.

Humans
glow in the dark.

In a desert,
the naked eye can see
the glow of a major city
from 125 miles away.

Snowflake, Arizona,
was founded in 1878 by two men
whose surnames were
Snow and Flake.

At the centre
of every snowflake is
a single piece of dust.

Claude Monet
paid a gardener to
dust his water lilies
before he painted them.

Van Gogh's
Olive Trees has a dead
grasshopper embedded
in the paint.

It is compulsory
for Dutch schoolchildren
to visit Rembrandt's paintings.

As a schoolboy,
legendary wrestler André the Giant
was driven to school by his neighbour,
the playwright Samuel Beckett.

Samuel Pepys
went to a performance of
Twelfth Night on Twelfth Night 1663,
and thought it was 'a silly play
and not relating at all
to the name or day'.

The West End
has fewer theatres
than London's private schools.

In 1907,
a riot broke out in New York
over a play in which a woman
drank a glass of beer.

Beer mats were originally
placed on top of glasses
to keep the dust out.

In the Second World War,
kegs of beer were flown to the
front line by Spitfire pilots.

One proposal to stop
plane hijackings to Cuba
in the 1970s was to build
a fake Havana airport
in south Florida.

In 2016,
a man from Wigan
sent a pie into space to promote
the World Pie Eating Championship.

A smartphone contains
more computing power than
the whole of NASA
had in 1969.

In 1985,
New York City had
2,000 mobile phones,
but only 12 of them
could be used at
any one time.

A man in New York
makes $500 a week collecting
fragments of gold and jewellery
from the city's pavements.

New York cabs
and Hertz rental cars
have yellow branding because
they were founded by the same man.

The flute
was invented
before the wheel.

Cement
was invented
before humans learned
to cook meat.

When Icelandic women
staged an equal-pay protest
by refusing to do any cooking,
all the supermarkets ran
out of sausages.

The world's
longest sausage
was 39 miles
long.

Volkswagen
sells more sausages
than cars.

The Lord Howe Island stick insect
is also known as the
'walking sausage'.

'Sausage guitar'
is urban slang for
air guitar played on
a stretched-out penis.

When Brian May goes on tour,
his guitar has its own
bodyguard.

In 2004,
Somalia issued a set
of guitar-shaped
coins.

In 2010,
the national mint of Chile
issued thousands of coins
stamped 'CHIIE'.

Goldman Sachs
complained to Microsoft
for autocorrecting their name to
Goddamn Sachs.

American Kitchen Foods
tried to rebrand peas by
shaping them into chips
and calling them
I Hate Peas.

Peas can be used
to treat constipation
in fish.

One-third of the fish
caught around the world
never get eaten.

During the Second World War,
fish-and-chip-shop managers were
exempt from military service.

The Russian
intelligence service
keeps Hitler's teeth
in a cigar box.

The UK
has 50,000
self-service tills.

British
trains arriving
up to nine minutes late
are counted as being on time.

In 2017,
a Japanese rail company
apologised after one of its trains
departed 20 seconds early.

590,000 Britons
turn up late for work each day,
costing the economy
£9 billion a year.

In Qin dynasty China,
the penalty for lateness
was death.

Mail theft in the US
was a capital offence
until 1872.

Until 1971,
the US Postmaster General
was last in the line of succession
to the presidency.

Donald Trump
is the first US president
in 168 years not to have a
pet in the White House.

US President
Zachary Taylor had never
voted in a presidential election
before he voted
for himself.

US President
William McKinley could
shake hands 50 times
a minute.

The world's
oldest footprints
are half a billion years old.

The first scientist
to study dinosaur footprints
thought they were made by
giant birds.

Archaeopteryx
was a bird-like dinosaur
that was too heavy to sit on
its own eggs without
cracking them.

The black feathers of the male
superb bird-of-paradise
absorb 99.95% of light.

The yellow-billed
oxpecker bird sleeps
in the armpit
of a giraffe.

Ancient Egyptians
used giraffes' tails
as fly swatters.

A male giraffe
drinks the urine
of a female giraffe
to see if she is ovulating.

Baby robins can
eat so many caterpillars
they turn green.

Baby guillemots
are called 'jumplings'.

Baby humpback whales
drink 150 gallons
of milk a day.

Female whales
have perforated umbilical cords
that snap off after birth so the baby
can swim to the surface
for its first breath.

When hibernating,
woodchucks breathe
as little as twice an hour.

Breathing the air
in New Delhi is equivalent
to smoking 45 cigarettes a day.

1 in 3 smartphones in India
run out of space every day because
millions of Indians send daily
'Good morning!' texts with
images or video attached.

In Honolulu,
it's illegal to
cross the street
using a mobile phone.

An Apple iPhone
contains more than half
the elements in the
periodic table.

Shoppers being absorbed in
their phones at the checkout
has resulted in a 15% fall
in chewing-gum sales.

Polyisobutylene
is the main ingredient
of chewing gum and
the inner tubes of
bicycle tyres.

A British designer has created
a chewing-gum recycling bin
made of recycled
chewing gum.

Chocolate
in the 16th century
was prescribed to treat
angina, constipation, dysentery,
indigestion, haemorrhoids,
flatulence and gout.

An 18th-century
remedy for headaches
was to comb the hair upwards,
stroking it with nutmeg
and vinegar.

19th-century doctors
advised growing a beard
to ward off illness.

15% of Americans
get sick from eating
food every year.

When Winston Churchill
visited the US during Prohibition,
he got a doctor's prescription for
an unlimited supply of alcohol.

Churchill's last words were:
'I'm bored with it all.'

The last king of Egypt
stole Winston Churchill's watch.

The last emperor of China
spent his final years as
a street sweeper.

37% of Britons think
their jobs are meaningless
and don't contribute to the world.

52% of Americans think
God is doing a
good job.

In ancient Egypt,
only gods and royalty
could eat marshmallows.

Pharaoh Rameses III
made an offering to the Nile god
of 11,998 jars of beans.

Pythagoras
died because he hated beans
and refused to run through
a field of them to escape
his murderers.

Socrates
enjoyed dancing.

Aristotle
had a lisp.

Karl Marx
spent more than
half his life in
England.

Thomas Young,
the first person to
decipher the Rosetta Stone,
had read the Bible twice
by the age of four.

The Bible
has no mention
of purgatory.

Utah has
a prison called the
Purgatory Correctional Facility.

Prisoners
in Brazil can have
their sentences reduced
by knitting.

Because Sweden is going cashless,
Swedish criminals have
been reduced to
stealing
owls.

Australian
Bassian thrushes
use their farts like leaf blowers
to uncover worms.

Giant predatory
hammerhead worms from Asia
are invading France.

At the time of the French Revolution,
only half the population of France
spoke French and only 1 in 8
could speak it well.

1 in 8
young Britons are
either bloggers
or vloggers.

Steve Jobs
never learned
to code.

The documentary
*Where in the World Is
Osama bin Laden?* was found
on Osama bin Laden's
computer.

Brian Eno used
an Apple Mac to compose
the start-up music for
Windows 95.

The most dangerous music
to play while driving is Wagner's
'Ride of the Valkyries'.

At the 1967 South African Grand Prix,
the Mexican national anthem
couldn't be found, so the
organisers played the
'Mexican Hat Dance'
instead.

The Czechoslovak national anthem
was the Czech national anthem
played between two halves of
the Slovak national anthem.

Chinese citizens
hearing their national anthem
are advised to stand still
but be full of energy.

The Sun generates
more energy in one second
than has been used during the
whole of human history.

The centre of the Sun
is 40,000 times hotter
than boiling water.

The strike of
a mantis shrimp is
so quick it makes the
surrounding water boil.

Mantis shrimp can see
a type of light that no other animals can,
and they use it to send each other
secret messages.

Puffins' beaks
glow in the dark.

Birds have
special feathers that
continually disintegrate into powder,
making their other feathers
waterproof.

Rolls-Royce Phantoms
have Teflon-coated umbrellas
installed in the doors.

A new umbrella drone
keeps you dry without you
having to hold it.

A *pluviophile* is
someone who loves
rainy days.

Malneirophrenia is
a bad mood caused by
a poor night's sleep.

Hexakosioihexekontahexaphobia
is the fear of the
number 666.

A *cumlin* is Scots for
a pet cat that decides
to go and live with
new owners.

In 19th-century Scotland,
to be counted as an island
a piece of land had to have
enough pasture to support
at least one sheep.

Depending on the definition,
the number of islands in the world
is somewhere between 86,000
and 7 billion.

Palmerston Atoll
in the South Pacific
has a population of 60,
all of whom speak with
a Gloucestershire accent.

Pheasant Island
is owned alternately
by France and Spain.

Pheasants are
more likely to be run over
than any other birds.

Pheasants will
stop attacking each other
if given spectacles.

Scottish football referees
are sponsored by
Specsavers.

The first advert
on Channel 5 was
for Chanel No. 5.

Perfume is
as bad for your health
as car exhaust.

A Californian company
has developed a perfume
to make cows smell like people,
so mosquitoes bite them instead of us.

Mosquitoes
are responsible
for half the deaths in
human history.

The quinine
in tonic water is
effective against malaria,
as long as you drink
300 gin and tonics
every day.

It's harder to tell
how drunk you are
if surrounded by
drunk people.

There are a dozen pubs
in the UK that claim to be
'Britain's oldest pub'.

'To be arrested by the white sergeant'
is 17th-century slang for
a man being hauled
out of a tavern
by his wife.

To stop postmen
loitering in ale houses,
they were given smart uniforms.

Posting a letter from
London to Edinburgh in 1818
cost as much as the average
daily wage.

Postage was
originally paid by the
person receiving the letter,
not the sender.

In 1909,
two suffragettes
posted themselves to
10 Downing Street to try to get
an audience with the prime minister.

The crowd that
greeted Tony Blair when
he first entered Downing Street
had been bussed in.

The winning tree in the
annual competition of the British
Christmas Tree Growers' Association
is displayed outside No. 10, and
the runner-up goes inside.

Artificial Christmas trees
are less environmentally friendly
than real ones, unless you
use them for more
than 20 years.

There is only one person
in the UK called
Mr Baubles.

There are 16 people in England
with the surname
Grinch.

The official names of
Scotland's salt-spreading trucks
include Sir Andy Flurry, Ready Spready Go
and Gritty Gritty Bang Bang.

Bin lorries in Taiwan
play music to alert residents
to bring out their rubbish.

7% of the land in Baku,
the capital of Azerbaijan,
is covered in rubbish dumps.

There are more than
180 tonnes of rubbish
on the Moon.

Every time
there's a full moon,
Sri Lanka has a public holiday.

In China,
public holidays last a week
because it takes so long to travel
across the country.

23 March is a
Bolivian public holiday
called The Day of the Sea, on which the
landlocked country mourns the loss
of its coastline in 1893.

Aston Martin has
developed a luxury
submarine.

The Icelandic for
'the cherry on top' is
rúsínan í pylsuendanum,
'the raisin at the end of the sausage'.

Laddie Boy,
President Warren Harding's dog,
not only went to state meetings,
he had his own chair.

A luxury hotel in Mexico
provides each guest with a
personalised sewing kit whose threads
match the clothes they're wearing.

The Bayeux Tapestry
is not a tapestry.

According to the
UK Department of Health,
the potato is not a vegetable.

Turkmenistan
has a public holiday to
celebrate melons.

The watermelon
is the state vegetable
of Oklahoma.

In the 19th century,
the US Supreme Court ruled
that tomatoes are
vegetables.

The oldest known mashed potatoes
were discovered in Utah and are
10,900 years old.

Climate change is
causing ancient mummies to
turn into black slime.

King Ferdinand I of Naples
had his enemies killed, stuffed,
mummified and mounted in
their everyday clothes.

Clothes are eaten by
only seven of the UK's
2,500 species
of moth.

There's a caterpillar
that eats coca leaves and
vomits cocaine onto
its predators.

Nematocampa caterpillars
hate being shouted at.

The 'shouting bomb',
developed by the US in 1957,
was designed to lecture the enemy
for three minutes as it
fell from the sky.

During the Second World War,
Foyle's bookshop bomb-proofed itself
by covering the roof with
copies of *Mein Kampf*.

Vellichor is the
strange wistfulness
of a second-hand bookshop.

Jólabókaflóð
is Iceland's official
book-buying season, which runs
from September to December.

Winners of the
Diagram Prize for the
'Oddest Book Title of the Year'
include *Living with Crazy Buttocks*
and *Cooking with Poo*.

Barbara Cartland
insisted on including the title
of every one of her 723 novels
in her *Who's Who* entry.

The library at
Balmoral is heated
by a two-bar electric fire.

Every year,
100 American fire fighters
are arrested for arson.

Fire fighters
used to shout
'Hi yi, hi yi, hi yi'
as they ran to a fire.

Fireman Sam's full name is
Samuel Peyton Jones.

Postman Pat's full name is
Patrick Clifton.

A petition to
change the name of
Bell End, in the West Midlands,
was called 'a bit silly' by
Stephen Young, 72, of
Minge Lane, Worcester.

The designer of the Spitfire
hated its name, saying,
'It's just the sort of
bloody silly name
they would choose.'

Dunkin' Donuts
is taking steps to
drop the word 'Donuts'
from its name.

Tunnock's teacakes
aren't allowed in RAF planes
in case they explode.

Bumblebees' penises
explode when they
ejaculate.

1% of middle-aged
honeybees work as
undertakers.

According to her last wishes,
Elizabeth Taylor arrived
late for her own
funeral.

Over 2 million people
went to Victor Hugo's funeral –
twice the population of
Paris at the time.

The population of Bangladesh
is 114% the size of Russia's,
crammed into an area
115 times smaller.

In 1926,
Poland gave the US
a 150th birthday card signed
by 20% of the population.

Inappropriate behaviour
on the Queen's Official Birthday
caused a goat that had reached the rank
of lance corporal in the British Army
to be demoted.

James Cook's goat
was the first known female
to have circumnavigated the globe.

Goats produce
more milk when listening to
'All I Want for Christmas Is You'.

The first Glastonbury tickets
cost £1 and came with a
free bottle of milk.

The Vatican uses milk
from the Pope's cows
to paint its buildings.

The Pope has eight titles,
and not one of them
is 'the Pope'.

Pope Formosus
died and was buried in 896,
but was dug up, tried
and found guilty
in 897.

Pope Francis
has his own 68-page
weekly magazine.

The person who writes
about legal marijuana
for *Forbes* magazine
is called Julie Weed.

Only two land animals
survive entirely on seaweed:
the North Ronaldsay sheep and
the Galapagos marine iguana.

Sea urchins
wear dead hermit crabs
as hats.

Straw hats in the US were
traditionally worn after 15 September;
any earlier and they would be
snatched off your head
and stomped on.

The earliest re-enactments
of the American Civil War took place
during the American Civil War.

During the American Civil War,
Ulysses S. Grant got so drunk
that he vomited into his
horse's mane.

In 1873,
the Spanish city of Cartagena
wrote to President Ulysses S. Grant
to ask to join the US.

The world's shortest
international bridge connects
Spain to Portugal and
is 3.2 metres long.

To travel between
the Portuguese towns
of Funchal and Monte you can
rent a toboggan.

Superionic ice
is both solid and liquid
at the same time.

The world's
hottest ice cream,
which contains peppers
100 times hotter than a jalapeño,
is called Devil's Breath and
is made in Glasgow.

The Scottish mountain
Bod an Deamhain, 'penis of the demon',
is usually translated into English
as The Devil's Point.

Titivillus
was a demon
blamed by medieval monks
for spelling misatkes.

Male proboscis monkeys are
more likely to attract a
large harem if they
have big noses.

Your nose looks
30% bigger in a selfie
than in a photo taken from
five metres away.

Robotic noses
smell more efficiently
if filled with
fake snot.

Saudi Arabia
was the first country
to grant citizenship
to a robot.

Senior citizens
in New Zealand can
join 'coffin clubs', where they
meet up once a week to make and
decorate their own coffins.

Homeless Victorians
could pay fourpence to
sleep in an unused coffin
for the night.

The first meat pies
were called
'coffins'.

Pie Town, New Mexico,
got its name when a prospector
who had failed to find gold
sold dried-fruit pies to
cowboys instead.

Albuquerque, New Mexico,
has a giant X-ray machine that
melts diamonds and makes electricity
that moves 20,000 times faster
than a bolt of lightning.

Lightning
produces
antimatter.

The Earth's
largest habitat
is the sky.

Baltimore has
'an eye in the sky'
that continually photographs
the city for the police.

Some police stations
in China use guard geese
instead of guard dogs.

In 1st-century Denmark,
rich people were buried with a chicken;
the very rich were buried
with a goose.

Che Guevara was
buried without his hands:
they were sent to Argentina
for fingerprinting.

God and Jesus are
the only characters in
The Simpsons to have
five fingers on
each hand.

10 out of the 12
water companies in the UK
still make use of
divining rods.

An underwater pipeline
discovered by border officials
in Kyrgyzstan in 2013 was used to
smuggle alcohol into the country
from Kazakhstan.

Kazakh engineers
have invented reusable
toilet paper.

British soldiers in the
Second World War had a ration of
three sheets of toilet paper a day.
US soldiers were allowed
22.5 sheets a day.

The penalty for taking
an unofficial photo during
the First World War was
death by firing squad.

During the Second World War,
Finnish frontline soldiers
were provided
with saunas.

When Peter III of Russia
caught a rat gnawing one
of his toy soldiers, he had it
court-martialled and hanged
on a miniature gallows.

Piglets prefer
new toys to ones
they've already
played with.

4,000 children
under the age of two
are listed as owners of
British companies.

The average child
has the aerobic fitness
of a triathlon athlete.

Harrods
used to sell
pet leopards.

The first pet cemetery
opened in Paris in 1899,
after the introduction of a
law that banned throwing
dead dogs into the Seine.

The first St Bernard
was called Barry.

Right-pawed dogs
are more cheerful than
left-pawed dogs.

It's easier to understand
sign language if the signer
is right-handed.

Scientists can tell
whether early humans
were left- or right-handed
by looking at their
fossilised teeth.

Pangolins
have no teeth;
they grind food in their stomachs
by swallowing small stones.

The Makira people
of the Solomon Islands
use flying-fox teeth
as currency.

Piranhas
continually replace
a quarter of their teeth
at a time.

Piranhas bark.

There's a train in Japan
that barks like a dog to
scare deer off the line.

Quaking
aspen trees
produce their own
sunscreen.

Pisonia trees
lure birds to their death
for no good reason.

Trees have
a very slow pulse,
expanding and contracting
to pump water round their body.

Horses
have five 'hearts':
each hoof acts as an extra
blood pump.

People who
walk slowly are
more likely to die
of heart disease.

Babies born in October are
more likely to live to 100 than
those born in March.

When a sperm
meets an egg and
conception takes place,
zinc atoms are released
and sparks literally fly.

A study at the
University of Illinois
has concluded that
sex doesn't sell.

Ted Hughes
was so attractive that
one woman who met him
had to rush straight to
the bathroom to be
physically sick.

John Wilkes Booth,
the man who shot Abraham Lincoln,
was dating five different women
when he himself was shot.

A sex pheromone found in
male mouse urine is named darcin,
after Mr Darcy.

Skúffuskáld is Icelandic for
someone who puts their poems
in a drawer rather than
publishing them.

Mbuki-mvuki is a Bantu word
for 'the irresistible urge to
strip when dancing'.

Sisu is Finnish for
'indomitable courage
and persistence in the
face of adversity'.

Uitwaaien is Dutch for
'to take a bracing walk
in the wind'.

Ancient Greek athletes
had their spleens removed
to help them to run faster.

The verb 'run'
has 645 meanings
in English.

At the 1932 Olympics,
the steeplechase lasted 8.5 laps
instead of the usual 7.5 because
officials lost track of how many times
the runners had been round.

In anonymous surveys,
half of all athletes
admit cheating.

The findings
of a 2015 study
about procrastination
were inconclusive because
half the participants didn't
get around to finishing
the survey.

The Procrastinators' Club of America
has earmarked 5 September as
Be Late for Something Day.

Neil Armstrong's
application to become an
astronaut arrived at NASA
a week after the deadline.

Neil Armstrong's spacesuit
had 21 layers and
weighed 36 kg.

NASA is designing
a clockwork rover for Venus:
the planet is so hot it would melt the
electronics in a normal one.

Three NASA astronauts
have appeared
in *Star Trek*.

The first series of *Star Trek* was made
by Lucille Ball's production company.
She originally thought it was a show
about celebrities on tour.

David Bowie
first appeared
on television aged 17, as the
founder of the Society for the
Prevention of Cruelty to
Long-Haired Men.

Men are
half as likely as women to
be naturally blond.

Pogonotrophy
is the cultivation
of a beard.

The entire British supply
of yak hair was used up
making false beards
for *The Hobbit*.

Peter the Great
introduced a beard tax for
everyone except clergy
and peasants.

In 1943,
the US banned
sliced bread.

20% of sandwich varieties
account for 80% of sales.

Prawn mayonnaise
has been Marks & Spencer's
bestselling sandwich
since 1981.

Mrs Beeton
had a recipe for a
toast sandwich.

Beetles
have become
20% smaller over
the last century.

The real-life policeman
who inspired *Sgt. Pepper*
didn't like The Beatles.

The police in Rome
have an undercover squad
that stops people jumping
in fountains.

A waterside restaurant in
Perth, Australia, hands out
water pistols so that diners
can repel the seagulls.

Australia
is slightly wider
than the Moon.

Australia is an island
20 times the size of Japan,
but with a shorter
coastline.

Galešnjak is
a heart-shaped island
in Croatia also known as
'the Island of Love'.

The average
heart rate in San Francisco
rose by four beats per minute
the day Donald Trump
was elected.

Holding hands causes
heart rates, breathing
and brainwaves
to synchronise.

Hand-dryers
in public toilets
blow faecal bacteria
all round the room
and spread it evenly
over your hands.

7% of Netflix users
watch movies in
public toilets.

The pig toilet,
once common in rural China,
fed human waste straight
to the pigs.

In Germany,
you can be fined €2,500
for calling someone an 'old pig'.

During the First World War,
truces would occasionally be called
in the trenches so both sides
could yell insults at
each other.

During the Christmas truce of 1914,
one English soldier got a haircut from
a German who used to be his
barber in Holborn.

In 1865,
the Duke of Buckingham
was blown from Holborn to Euston
through a pneumatic tube
intended for parcels.

Roman maps
gave exact distances between towns
and rated the roadside inns
and the road quality.

In Iceland,
drawing a map on an envelope
works just as well as writing
the address.

Until 2011,
buildings in South Korea
were numbered according to
when they were built.

When the River Han in Korea
was crossed by tightrope walkers,
the *Washington Post* reported:
'Skywalkers in Korea
Cross Han Solo'.

The Yellow River in China has
lost 30% of its fish species,
and 66% of its water
is undrinkable.

Only 36%
of Americans
can locate North Korea
on a map.

There are
Google Maps for the
Moon, Mercury, Venus, Mars, Pluto,
four of Jupiter's moons and
seven of Saturn's.

One of the moons
of Uranus is called
Margaret.

Uranus is
the coldest planet
in the Solar System,
even though it's nearer
to the Sun than Neptune.

99% of the time,
the temperature on Mars
is below zero.

Mars has distanced itself
from the deep-fried Mars bar
because it goes against the company's
'commitment to promoting
healthy, active lifestyles'.

There is
a pig farm in Japan
where the pigs only drink
green tea.

Over half
the farmworkers
in the US work
in Texas.

The most
common job in
America today is
shop assistant.

Shops in Romania may
offer chewing gum instead
of small change.

Kraft Foods in China
tried replacing the filling
in Oreo biscuits with
chewing gum, but it
didn't catch on.

In 2005,
a red panda called Babu
escaped from a nature reserve in
Birmingham and was voted
'Brummie of the Year'.

When a new motorway bisected
the HP Sauce factory in Birmingham,
a pipeline was installed that carried
vinegar from one side of the road
to the sauce-mixing department
on the other.

Noisy miners
are small birds of the
honeyeater family.

Vulture bees
make honey from
rotten meat.

If butterflies eat road salt,
the males become more muscular
and the females get bigger
eyes and brains.

Passion-fruit vines
deter butterflies from laying eggs
on their leaves by growing
mock butterfly eggs.

Martha's Vineyard,
Massachusetts, is home
to a tiny frog called
a pinkletink.

Tiny moons
in Saturn's rings
named after kittens include
Fluffy, Garfield, Socks, Whiskers,
Butterball and Mittens.

Journalist
Christopher Morley
called his two cats Shall and Will,
because 'nobody can tell
them apart'.

Lyndon B. Johnson
had two beagles called
Him and Her.

When Gavin Williamson
was Conservative chief whip,
he kept a tarantula called Cronus
on his desk.

Spiders have
hydraulic legs.

The first hydraulic lift
was used to carry
sheep onto a roof.

If you lift
a kangaroo's tail
off the ground,
it can't hop.

Almost 10%
of a cat's bones
are in its tail.

Luna moths avoid
being eaten by bats
by using their tails as
sonar deflectors.

The odds of being bitten
by a shark, bear or snake
in any three-year period is
893 quadrillion to one.

Lima bean plants
attacked by spider mites
release a burst of chemicals that
attract insects which then
eat the spider mites.

The tea mite,
Tuckerella japonica,
has been lurking in
cups of tea for
3,000 years.

There's only
one species of
tea plant.

Tea leaves uncurl
when hot water is poured on them,
in a process known as the
'agony of the leaves'.

The world's largest amphibian
makes a sound like
a crying baby.

The call of the
male túngara frog of
Central America sounds like
a *Star Trek* phaser.

Parrots use Alexa
to order items
from Amazon.

When ducks sleep in a row,
the ones at either end sleep
with their outside eye open,
looking for predators.

Fish swim faster
in city rivers than in
country rivers.

The first English reference
to fish-and-chip shops called them
'a considerable source
of nuisance'.

Shops sell more clothes
if their mannequins
have a head.

Shrews' heads are
20% bigger in the summer
than in winter.

The pen-tailed tree shrew's
entire diet is fermented nectar
containing up to
3.8% alcohol.

Alcohol
helps you speak
foreign languages better.

The International
Bartenders Association
recognises only
77 cocktails.

One of the pilgrims
on the *Mayflower* sailed with
139 pairs of shoes.

First names of pilgrims
on the *Mayflower* included
Remember, Resolve,
Humility, Truelove
and Wrestling.

When the royal family changed its name
in 1917 because it was too German,
new names considered included
Guelph, Wipper, Wettin,
Tudor-Stuart and
England.

The royal family is
named after Windsor Castle.

A man in Rio has
lived in a sandcastle
since 1996.

Saturn's moon Titan
has electrostatic sand that
would be perfect for
sandcastles.

The world's largest sandcastle
was built in Germany,
180 km from
the coast.

You can be fined
€1,000 for taking sand
from Sardinia.

In 2018,
after a nine-year legal battle,
an unemployed man in southern Italy
was acquitted of stealing
an aubergine.

The Lamborghini
Countach gets its name from
the Piedmontese slang
for 'Holy shit!'

There has been
only one posthumous
Formula 1 champion.

Mexico City's
Day of the Dead parade
didn't exist until it appeared in
the James Bond film *Spectre*.

The phrase 'vital statistics'
originally referred to births,
marriages and deaths.

George Washington is the
highest-ranking general in the US,
even though he's been dead
for over 200 years.

George Washington
called a ceasefire during the
American Revolutionary War to
return a British general's terrier that
had wandered onto the battlefield.

King Henry III of France
liked to tie a ribbon round his neck,
from which he hung a basket
of small dogs.

Dogs
like reggae.

Animals and humans
prefer music that is
close to their own
vocal range.

A mathematical study
of 50 years of hit singles
concluded that The Beatles
had no influence at all on
the history of pop music.

Ozzy Osbourne's 1992 tour
was called 'No More Tours'.
His 2018 tour was called
'No More Tours 2'.

The Tour de France
hasn't been won by
a French cyclist
since 1985.

Chinese tourists
can pay $50,000
to shoot a polar bear
in Canada.

A Chinese robot named
Xiaoyi ('Little Doctor') has
passed the written stage of the
national medical licensing exam.

Ford has a
robot called Robutt
that simulates a large man
sitting on its car seats.

Speeding offences
increase significantly
the weekend after the release
of a *Fast and the Furious* film.

The video game
Grand Theft Auto V
has made more money
than any film in history.

Psycho
was the first
major American film
to feature a flushing toilet.

The boy who
played Piggy in
Lord of the Flies
was bullied by
the other boys.

The first eight popes
were all murdered.

There is a secret passageway
at the back of the Vatican in case
the Pope needs to escape.

Pope Urban VIII
issued a decree that
all pasta shops must be
at least 25 yards apart.

Italian pasta-makers
used to knead dough
with their bare feet.

The word 'shampoo'
comes from a Hindi word
meaning 'to knead'.

The Indian peafowl
is the national bird of India.
The Great Indian Bustard nearly
made it, but there were
concerns it might
be misspelled.

Melville Dewey,
creator of the Dewey Decimal System,
was such a fan of spelling reform that
he spelled his first name 'Melvil'.

Hotmail is so named because
it contains the letters HTML:
it was originally HoTMaiL.

When Bill Clinton
was president, he sent
only two emails.

The man who
invented email
later became an importer
of sheep semen.

Human semen
contains fructose.

Scientists have devised a method
of finding the best sperm for IVF
by making them complete a
tiny obstacle course.

In the first
egg-and-spoon race, in 1894,
competitors had to punt
with their spare hand.

In 2018,
a charity snail race was
cancelled after cold weather
caused all the competitors
to go into hibernation.

Sea slugs
prefer to eat an animal
that has just eaten another animal,
so they get two meals in one.

The UK's food supply chain means
we are only ever nine meals away
from empty supermarket
shelves.

Some bacteria are
not only resistant to antibiotics,
they enjoy eating them.

The Korowai people of New Guinea
put grubs in their ears to
eat their earwax.

Dinosaurs suffered
from dandruff.

People suffering
from plague may not
enter a library
in the UK.

The Queen is a
fee-paying member of
the Jigsaw Puzzle Library.

The Queen owns a treadmill
that 18 horses can use
at the same time.

Scientists have
made a hat for horses
with built-in earphones
so they can listen to music.

Using a musical instrument
to annoy someone is
illegal in Singapore.

Pangolin-and-caterpillar
soup is illegal
in China.

Carp soup is a popular
Christmas dish in Poland.
It's good luck to keep the scales
in your wallet till the
next Christmas.

The Christmas Tree Grower
Council of Europe holds its
Christmas party in June.

The first person to
use the phrase 'Merry Christmas'
was also the first to use
the word 'Prosecco'.

In the last 300 years,
the average size of a wine glass
has increased almost sevenfold.

Jeff Goldblum
puts orange juice
on his cereal.

The Pope
drives a blue
Ford Focus.

Ísbíltúr is Icelandic for
going for a drive and ending up
with an ice cream.

Eating
ice cream
for breakfast can
increase mental alertness.

1 in 5 Britons
cannot name a single
author of literature.

The first, second and third
most common sentences in
Stephenie Meyer's *Twilight* novels
are 'I sighed', 'He sighed'
and 'I shrugged.'

George Orwell
ran the village shop in
Wallington, Hertfordshire.

Agatha Christie
worked as a hospital
pharmacy assistant during
the First World War.

The first real murder
on the Orient Express
took place the year after
Agatha Christie's novel came out.

King Ferdinand of Bulgaria
was so scared of being murdered
on the Orient Express that he
locked himself in the toilet.

The surrender of Germany
after the First World War and
the surrender of France in the
Second World War were signed in
the same carriage of the Orient Express.

Theodore Roosevelt
coined the expression
'lunatic fringe'.

When Frinton-on-Sea, Essex,
got its first pub in 2000, locals
described it as the worst thing
to hit the town since
the Luftwaffe.

The oldest known writing
on Earth contains
a swastika.

In ancient Greek,
one line of text would be
written left to right, and
the next right to left.

There used to be
six more letters in
the English alphabet:
'eth', 'thorn', 'wynn',
'yogh', 'ash' and
'ethel'.

Denmark hated
the letter 'Q' so much
they abolished it in 1872.

The letters 'K', 'W' and 'Y'
were officially added to the
Portuguese alphabet in 2009.

Seychelles
is the only member of the UN
whose name has no letters
in common with
'Britain'.

Britain and Portugal
have been allies
since 1373.

A Portuguese way of
telling someone to leave you alone is:
'Go away and comb monkeys.'

'To feed the donkey sponge cake'
is a Polish expression meaning
'to treat someone better
than they deserve'.

'Don't come the
raw prawn with me'
is Australian slang for
'You must be joking.'

Prawn crackers in
Italian are *nuvole di drago*,
'dragon clouds'.

Some buildings in Hong Kong
have large holes designed
into them for dragons
to fly through.

The world's largest building
in the shape of a bottle is the
Strong Drinks Museum
in Moldova.

A *hecatompedon* is
a building measuring
exactly 100 ft by 100 ft.

The lost property office
at Dublin airport has an
unclaimed tombstone with the words:
'You will always be remembered,
never forgotten.'

The Chinese government
has announced a crackdown
on strippers at funerals.

The classic ghost costume
dates from the time when bodies of
the poor were wrapped in a sheet.

Highwayman Thomas Wilmot
used to disguise himself as a ghost,
scare gamblers from the tables,
then take the money
they'd left behind.

Gambling was illegal
in public libraries from
1898 to 2005.

In 2014,
Oakland, California,
discovered that pinball had been
illegal there for 80 years and
immediately legalised it.

In 2017,
Oregon banned poker
and also a game called
Big Injun, despite the fact that
it hadn't been played
since the 1950s.

The best poker face
is a smile.

Blind people smile,
even though they have
never seen anyone
else doing so.

When Wal-Mart opened in Germany,
it scrapped its policy of employees
smiling at customers because
the Germans found it
too weird.

In Germany, until 1888
you had to have a licence
to take a child out in a pram.

The German for
'contraceptive pill'
is *Antibabypille*.

STEVE is an acronym for
the path sperm take through
the male reproductive system:
Seminiferous Tubules, Epididymis,
Vas deferens, Ejaculatory duct.

'Popeye biceps' and 'Popeye butt'
are medical terms for muscle injuries.

Blood pressure readings
are 50% more accurate
when taken at home.

When a white coat
is worn and people are
told it belongs to a doctor,
they become more attentive.
It doesn't work if they
are told it belongs
to a painter.

Hay fever didn't exist
until the 1800s.

There is a conspiracy theory
that Finland doesn't exist and
was made up by Japan
and the USSR.

The existence
of Antarctica was
completely unknown
until 1820.

Queen Victoria
didn't know that
pandas existed.

It costs five times more
to keep a panda than
an elephant.

Humans and bees
are the only species
elephants fear.

Pliny the Elder
noted that the stare of
a menstruating woman
could kill bees.

Spot removal
for Pliny the Elder
involved rubbing the affected part
with a paste made from the
ashes of a roast dolphin.

Black leopards
have spots, but you
can only see them in
infrared light.

Puma
and Adidas were
founded by two brothers who
fell out and went into competition
against one another.

After 11 months
on the International Space Station,
astronaut Scott Kelly returned to Earth
13 milliseconds younger than
his twin brother.

Ewan McGregor's brother
used to be a Tornado pilot who flew
with the call sign 'Obi-Two'.

The Porgs in *Star Wars*
were devised to cover up the
vast numbers of puffins that
kept walking into shot.

There are eight places on Earth
called Puffin Island.

The Alutiiq people of Alaska
made rattles from
puffin's beaks.

Alaska has
1,000 earthquakes
a month.

At Seattle's 1909
Alaska–Yukon–Pacific Exposition,
one of the raffle prizes was
a month-old orphan
named Ernest.

The 2017 Ig Nobel Prize for Cognition
was awarded to scientists who proved
that identical twins often can't tell
which of them is which.

In 2007,
the Ivory Coast government
gave away a house to an employee
as a prize for turning up on time.

More than 50% of
the ivory imported into China
comes from woolly
mammoths.

10 million mammoths
are still trapped in the
Arctic permafrost.

Frostproof, Florida,
was so named to persuade
farmers it wouldn't get a frost.
Two years later, frost killed almost
its whole citrus crop.

Whynot, North Carolina,
was named after a long debate
concluded with someone saying:
'Why not just name it Why Not
and let's go home?'

Johnny Cash's
real name is J. R. Cash:
his parents couldn't agree
on his names, only the initials.

Johnny Cash named
his daughter Roseanne after
Rose and Anne, his nicknames for
her mother's breasts.

UK street names include
Fanny Hands Lane,
Willey Lane and
Uranus Road.

Houses on streets
with rude names
are cheaper.

You can say 'f*ck' at any time
on Canadian radio, provided it's
a French-language station.

NASA has
its own radio station
called Third Rock Radio.

In 1972,
Peru banned Santa Claus
from appearing on
radio and TV.

Santa's helpers in Iceland include
the Spoon Licker, the Door Sniffer
and the Sausage Swiper.

Good Icelandic children
get presents at Christmas,
naughty ones get rotten potatoes.

Frederick William of Prussia
decreed that anyone refusing
to plant potatoes would have
their noses and ears cut off.

Police in Vanuatu are
encouraging people to grow
potatoes instead of pot.

It is illegal in England
to import Polish potatoes,
or potatoes suspected
of being Polish.

When foreign films
are dubbed into Polish,
all the parts, even those of
women and children,
are read by one
male actor.

During a speech in Warsaw,
Jimmy Carter mistakenly announced
he wanted to have sex with
the Polish people.

Richard Nixon's chair
in the Cabinet Room was
2.5 inches higher than
everyone else's.

Teddy Roosevelt
had a pet badger
called Josiah.

In 2017,
a Tyneside woman
found a cyst in the ear
of her beagle that bore an
uncanny resemblance
to Donald Trump.

Trumpadóir is
Irish for 'loudmouth'.

People with
autotopagnosia
literally cannot tell
their arse from their elbow.

A *macroverbumsciolist* is
someone who pretends to know a word,
but then secretly looks it up.

A *wonty-tump* is
Herefordshire dialect
for a 'molehill'.

George Orwell's
first word was
'beastly'.

Fantastic Beasts and Where to Find Them
won the Oscar for Best Costume Design,
the only Harry Potter film to win
an Academy Award.

The fact that the
Defence Against the Dark Arts
professors in *Harry Potter* are all
cursed was inspired by all the
drummers in *Spinal Tap*
dying in bizarre ways.

The JD in JD Wetherspoon is from
a character in *The Dukes of Hazzard*;
Wetherspoon was a teacher at
the founder's primary school.

The Irish
get through 50 beer mats
per person per year.

The Queen
owns several pubs,
including one called
the Windsor Castle.

The Queen has won
more than £6 million
from horse racing.

The Queen
employs an official
stamp collector.

1930s postboxes
doubled as stamp vending
machines.

In 1972,
Bhutan issued
a set of talking stamps.

'Philately' is
from the Greek for
the 'love of exemption
from taxation'.

In Mexico,
artists can pay their taxes
by donating their work.

The US tax code
has increased in length
from 400 pages in 1913
to 70,000 pages today.

Denmark
taxes new cars
at 150%.

Until 1999,
tax-deductible items in
Germany included
bribes.

Germany's
Rheinsberg nuclear plant
was decommissioned in 1990 but
still has over 100 employees.

In 2008,
two pigeons at an
Iranian nuclear facility
were arrested for spying.

US civil defence guidelines
advise against using
hair conditioner
after a nuclear
strike.

Reed College in Oregon has
the world's only nuclear reactor
run by undergraduates.

The first nuclear reactor
was built in a squash court.

Tennis courts
were once shaped
like an hourglass.

The grass at Wimbledon is
trimmed by a millimetre a week
for 12 weeks and cared for
by a man called
Mr Stubley.

Ritalin was named
after its inventor's wife Rita
because it improved her
tennis so much.

Tennys Sandgren is a
tennis player from
Tennessee.

There's a street in Leeds
called Cavalier Approach.

The Laughing Cavalier
isn't laughing and isn't
dressed as a cavalier.

Gainsborough
painted his outdoor scenes
using little models made of broccoli.

In 2003,
the Tate announced that
two Turner paintings of Venice
were actually of Portsmouth.

'Dockyard oyster'
is a phrase used in Portsmouth
to describe a gob of phlegm
on the pavement.

The street price
of a hand grenade in
Sweden is 100 krona,
or £8.62.

Wounds sustained
during the day heal
twice as quickly as those
sustained at night.

Pieces of coconut shell
were used by Pacific Islanders
to mend broken skulls.

Mahler's
Sixth Symphony
features a part for an
enormous hammer.

Picasso liked
to shoot blanks at
people who bored him.

Bangladesh is home to
the world's only specialist
diarrhoea hospital.

1 in 3
people in Britain
admitted to hospital as an
emergency have at least
five illnesses.

The 911 emergency number
used to be spoken as 'nine–eleven'
but was restyled as 'nine–one–one'
to avoid people wasting time
looking for the '11' button.

The phonebook on
Norfolk Island, Australia,
lists people by their nicknames.

Tancítaro, Mexico,
has a special police unit
to stamp out avocado theft.

In 2017,
Frankfurt police
found a car belonging to
a 76-year-old man who had
forgotten where he parked it
20 years earlier.

Pittsburgh police
classify condoms as
'instruments of crime'
to help them prosecute
sex workers.

A single sex act
by parasitic flukeworms
can last for over
40 years.

When two
earthworms mate,
they both have
children.

Castrator pea crabs
live inside the genitals
of limpets.

Chinese street barbers
shave the insides of their
customers' eyelids.

20–20 vision
is not perfect,
just normal.

The only things
anyone has ever 'seen'
are photons.

Sea urchins are
the only known animals
that can see without
having eyes.

Your eardrums move
in sync with your eyeballs,
but no one knows why.

Lobsters use sand
in their inner ear to
work out if they are
the right way up.

Until the mid-1800s,
lobsters were considered to be
food for the poor.

30,000 years ago,
people ate mammoth
and fed reindeer
to their dogs.

10,000 years ago,
lions didn't have
manes.

African wild dogs
vote on whether to go
hunting or not
by sneezing.

The Isle of Man was
the first place in the world
to give votes to women
and under-18s.

The king of
the Isle of Man
from 1112 to 1143 was
Olaf the Titbit.

Gavin Barwell,
former MP and author of
How to Win a Marginal Seat,
lost his marginal seat.

Applause
is forbidden inside
the Houses of Parliament.

Police guarding the outside of
the Houses of Parliament are
under orders to feel inside
men's underpants.

In 1930s New Zealand,
there was an outbreak of
exploding trousers.

During the First World War,
an estimated one tonne of explosives
was fired for every square metre
on the Western Front.

The Western Front
was supplied with
500 ferrets a month
to catch rabbits.

Rabbits
are repelled by
the butterfly bush.

The skunk cabbage
melts the frozen ground
around it by generating
heat like an animal.

When the retired Roman emperor
Diocletian was asked to
return to the throne,
he said he'd rather
grow cabbages.

The entire Roman Empire
was sold at auction
in 193 AD.

Christie's auctioneers
are taught to stop their
hands shaking with nerves by
clenching their buttocks.

In 1942,
a single banana was
auctioned in London for
the equivalent of £95.

Japanese farmers have created
a new kind of banana
with edible peel.

Farmers in India
use Coca-Cola as a pesticide:
the sugar attracts ants that
eat the larvae that
would have eaten
the crops.

Wolf whistles were
first used by Albanian farmers
to warn sheepdogs of
approaching wolves.

Some Scottish farmers
use lasers to protect
their livestock
from eagles.

Laser pointers are
the second most common
cause of pilot incapacity,
after tummy upsets.

There are more
living US astronauts
than living Concorde pilots.

The wingspan of a Boeing 747
is longer than the distance travelled
during the Wright brothers'
first flight.

The first successful
all-metal passenger plane
had wickerwork seats.

A group of raptors
in flight is called
a 'kettle'.

A group of penguins
on land is called
a 'waddle'.

A group of sharks
is called a 'shiver'.

A group of swans
on land is called
a 'bank'.

Deutsche Bank's
largest shareholder
is Chinese.

China has an exact replica
of the Austrian village of Hallstatt
so tourists don't have to go
all that way to see it.

Palau
is to pass a new law
allowing only five-star hotels
to be built.

A hotel in Oman
employs a full-time
turtle ranger.

The Mary River turtle
breathes through
its genitals.

Plankton
were one of the
12 official logos for
Eurovision 2018.

If food supplies to Britain in
the Second World War had been
cut off completely, there were plans
for everyone to eat plankton.

Phytoplankton
are microscopic plants
that produce up to 85%
of the planet's oxygen.

Oxygen levels
in a human womb
are similar to those at
the top of Mount Everest.

The cornea is the
only part of the human body
with no blood supply.
It gets its oxygen
from the air.

The ancient Greeks
believed the uterus
wandered around
inside the body.

Examining
the pelvis is the
only way to tell the
sex of a human skeleton.

No one knows if Lucy,
humanity's oldest ancestor,
was male or female.

Male red-sided garter snakes
pretend to be female and entice
other males to have sex with them.

To kill off the snakes in Guam,
2,000 dead mice were pumped full
of paracetamol and dropped by
tiny parachutes into the forests.

Parachute tester
Rickster Powell has made
20,000 parachute jumps and
tested 50 new parachutes –
only nine of which went
into production.

The Guinness World Record
for the highest fall survived
without a parachute
is 10,000 metres.

The world record
for the most people
licking ice cream in
one place is 2,728.

The world record
for the most people
licking lollipops
is 12,831.

'Lick into shape' comes
from the medieval belief that
bear cubs were born shapeless
and were 'licked into shape'
by their mothers.

Matabele ants
nurse each other and
tend each other's wounds.

Ancient ants
were the size
of hummingbirds.

Palaeontologists lick stones
to identify whether they
are fossils or not.

The longest-ever dog's tongue
was more than twice as long
as the smallest living dog.

The world's largest
timber-framed structure
is a replica of Noah's Ark at
a Christian theme park
in Kentucky.

In 2004,
a boat in Texas
capsized because everyone
ran to one side to look
at a nudist beach.

In 2012,
a smuggler was arrested at
the Smuggler's Inn, Washington,
after arriving in a car with the
licence plate SMUGLER.

Seven US states have
not produced a single billionaire.

The famous sign
'Welcome to Fabulous Las Vegas'
isn't in Las Vegas but in
Paradise, Nevada.

There are more rooms in
the Bellagio hotel in Las Vegas
than there are people in the
town of Bellagio in Italy.

It's illegal for
citizens of Monaco
to go to the casino
at Monte Carlo.

The first
James Bond film
was released on the
same day as the
first Beatles single.

Paul McCartney
met John Lennon at
a church fete.

The first picnics
took place
indoors.

In Thailand,
you can be arrested
for having a picnic.

A typical British family
with children throws away
40% of the food it buys.

The average American
lives 18 miles from
his or her mother.

Mother's Day is
banned in North Korea
because it distracts citizens
from their love for
Kim Jong-un.

Jim Henson's mother
owned the green coat that
the original Kermit the Frog's
skin was made from.

A frozen wood frog
goes completely rigid;
when you drop one,
it goes 'clink'.

The pumpkin toadlet
is a Brazilian frog whose
mating call can be heard by
every animal except other
pumpkin toadlets.

The Cuyaba dwarf frog
inflates its bottom to
scare off predators.

The Aztecs
burned incense
to mask the smell of
the Spanish.

King Henry IV of France
smelled strongly
of goat.

Beyoncé
has released
more perfumes
than albums.

Will Young
considered breaking his leg
to get out of *Strictly Come Dancing*.

The oldest member of
England's 2018 World Cup squad
was Ashley Young.

The oldest member of
any 2018 World Cup squad was
Egyptian goalkeeper Essam El-Hadary.
He was born in Kafr al-Battikh
– 'Town of the Watermelon' –
and celebrates victory by
eating watermelons.

Blue whales eat
four tonnes of
krill a day.

The Sami people
of Lapland have
werewhales, not
werewolves.

To prepare for
the role of Wolverine,
Hugh Jackman researched wolves,
not realising they were
different animals.

Moose
is Scots for
'mouse'.

3D-printed
mouse penises can
alert airport security scanners.

In 2017,
a man at Colombo airport
was arrested for attempting
to smuggle almost a kilo
of gold in his rectum
'with difficulty'.

Military
special services
reserve difficult tasks
for soldiers aged 27 or older.

The French
work a 35-hour week
and finish their tasks by
Thursday lunchtime.

Seamus Heaney
was scared of frogs.

Lenin
spoke English
with an Irish accent.

The 'transatlantic' accent used
by Katharine Hepburn and Cary Grant
was invented by their
dialect coach.

The first director of *Jaws* was
fired because he kept
calling the shark
a whale.

In the film *Twister*,
the noise of the tornado
was made using
the moan of
a camel.

Angela Merkel
has an ambition
to host her own
TV talk show.

Sooty and Soo
weren't allowed to
touch each other on TV
in case things got steamy.

The first US TV show
broadcast in the Soviet Union
was *Fraggle Rock*.

In 1990,
the Soviet Union paid for
$3 billion worth of Pepsi
with warships.

Coca-Cola, Pepsi and Dr Pepper
were all invented
by pharmacists.

French pharmacists
are all qualified to identify
edible mushrooms.

Mushrooms are farmed
in the catacombs
under Paris.

There are 19
alligator farms
in the US.

70% of all
the birds on Earth
are farmed poultry.

Clarence Birdseye
founded his company with $7,
which he spent on blocks of ice
and an electric fan.

The president of Rwanda
is an Arsenal fan.

The women's football World Cup
has only ever been won
by democracies.

Fund managers
from poor backgrounds
are better at investing than
those from wealthy backgrounds.

When investor
Henry Budd died in 1862,
he left his fortune to his two sons,
on condition that neither
of them ever grew
a moustache.

The three
richest Americans
have as much money as the
160 million poorest Americans.

Due to climate change,
Sweden's Lake of the Pine Trees
is now surrounded by
birch trees.

53 million years ago,
Antarctica was covered in
palm trees.

There is a species of palm tree
that can walk.

The cabbage palm tree
is neither a cabbage, a palm
nor a tree.

Palm cockatoos
make drum kits out of
seedpods and sticks.

T-Rex
couldn't stick its
tongue out.

Everyone
has a unique
tongue print.

The printer on the
International Space Station was
20 years old when it was
replaced in 2018.

Google
accounts for
40% of the Internet's
carbon footprint.

The world's
smallest computer is
smaller than a grain of sand.

The hard drive
on Terry Pratchett's computer
containing his unfinished works
was destroyed at his request
by a steamroller.

In 2017,
a drink-driver in Northern Ireland
was arrested after his Ford Fiesta
phoned the police to say it had
been involved in a crash.

An AI programmed to
come up with messages for
Love Hearts sweets suggested
'BEAR WIG', 'MEAT MATE' and
'YOU ARE BAG'.

Messages in the first sticks of rock
included 'Do you love me?',
'Do you love sprats?' and
'Sir Robert Peel'.

Names of bell-ringing peals include
the 'Reverse Canterbury Pleasure',
the 'Yorkshire Surprise' and the
'I Can't Believe It's Not Yorkshire
Surprise'.

There is a bell
that's been ringing in Oxford
non-stop for 178 years.

The first
ice-hockey referees
used cowbells, not whistles.

The first
ice-hockey pucks were
made from frozen
cow dung.

The first
American footballs
were meant to be spherical;
they just weren't blown
up properly.

The first
rubber bands
were made from the
inner tubes of
car tyres.

The minty flavour
of toothpaste comes
from pine trees.

Colgate
has trademarked
the Tooth Fairy.

Lloyd's of London
insured Ken Dodd's teeth
for four times more than
they did the *Titanic*.

Tetley tea's
chief tester has
his taste buds insured
for £1 million.

There were more
coffee houses per person
in London in the 1700s
than there are today.

The man who
invented coffee pods
doesn't use them because
they're bad for the
environment.

In ancient China,
adulterous men were
punished by having their
penises removed.

25% of Americans
have had a pubic hair
grooming injury.

'Gooseberry bush'
was 19th-century slang
for 'pubic hair'.

'Got the morbs' was
Victorian slang for
'temporary melancholia'.

'Muffin-walloper' was
Victorian slang for
a 'gossip'.

'Loitersacke' was
17th-century slang for
a 'slacker'.

Argon
is Greek for 'lazy'.

When the chemical compound
thioacetone was first distilled,
it smelled so bad that it caused
anyone within a mile of the lab
to vomit and fall unconscious.

Scientists can't tell
what sex a person is by
studying their brain alone.

By swabbing
your phone screen,
a researcher can find out
what you eat, where you've been
and what medicine you take.

The World Mobile Phone
Throwing Championships
take place in Finland.

When the Russians
invaded Finland in 1940,
they were so sure they'd be
welcomed that they brought
musical instruments
with them.

During the war between
India and Pakistan in 1947,
King George VI was technically
at war with himself.

Pakistan was originally Pakstan,
an acronym representing Punjab,
Afghan province, Kashmir,
Sindh and Baluchistan.

Karachi bid for
the 1960 Winter Olympics,
despite its temperature never
having fallen below 0°C.

When the 1964 Winter Olympics
were threatened by lack of snow,
the Austrian Army carried
40,000 cubic metres of it
up to the ski slopes.

When the East German luge team
were caught heating the runners on
their sleds in 1968, they blamed
a 'capitalist revanchist plot'.

Liechtenstein only found out
they had the same flag as Haiti
when they both arrived
at the 1936 Olympics.

According to
the US Flag Code,
the Stars and Stripes
is a living thing.

The current 50-star US flag
was designed in 1958 by
a 17-year-old as part
of a school project.
He got a B.

A retired UN official
has spent 25 years collecting
14,000 'Do Not Disturb' signs.

The official
retirement age
for Russian men is
two years above their
average life expectancy.

Alzheimer's
cannot be definitively diagnosed
until the patient is dead.

Jason Bourne
is named after Ansel Bourne,
one of the most famous amnesiacs
in medical history.

Type A and Type B
personalities were made up
by a tobacco company.

Smoking
the venom of the
Sonoran Desert toad
is said to be like having
a Force 5 hurricane
in your head.

Scientists in Morocco have
created a scorpion-milking machine
that can extract venom from
four scorpions at once.

The man who
invented condensed milk
also invented an amphibious
horse and cart equipped
with a mast and sail.

Grampussing was a punishment
in which sailors' hands were tied above
their heads and buckets of water
poured down their sleeves.

The heatproof sleeve
on the outside of a disposable
coffee cup is called a 'zarf'.

DEFRA gets through 1,400 disposable
cups a day.

69
ants' nests
in the UK have
listed building status.

UK Control of Noise
at Work Regulations (2006)
recognise no distinction
between a factory and
an opera house.

The Ministry of Defence's
official *Book of Abbreviations*
is 373 pages long.

Perissology
is the unnecessary use of rather
more words than are necessary
to get the meaning of the words
across to the majority of people
in a meaningful manner or way.

A *philodox*
is someone who loves
their own opinion.

To *perendinate* is
to put something off
till the day after
the day after
tomorrow.

Parorexia is
the desire to eat
strange foods.

Britain's leading
apple researcher is
severely allergic to apples.

The US once had
over 14,000 varieties of apple.
Today, there are only 90.

The original
Bramley apple tree
has a fan club
in Japan.

iTunes customers
have to agree not to
use Apple products to
create nuclear weapons.

MPs in the
Ukrainian parliament
must leave weapons and explosives
in their lockers.

MPs in the
UK parliament are
not allowed to call each other
asses, gits, rats, sods, swine, idiots,
tarts, cowards, hooligans
or guttersnipes.

The Habeas Corpus Act (1679)
became law only because a portly lord
was counted as 10 votes and the
Opposition didn't notice.

The British Labour Party is
the largest political party
in western Europe.

The Romans
drank turpentine to
treat depression.

Frankincense
is used in Oman as a
stomach soother, cough medicine,
blood thinner, wound cleaner
and fly repellent.

King Edward VII had
a liqueur specially created
for him to drink while driving.

Prairie voles can
drink the equivalent
of 15 bottles of
wine a day.

A group of pandas
is called an 'embarrassment'.

The man who invented
the plastic garden flamingo
dressed in matching clothes with
his wife for 35 years.

26 tons of clothing
are abandoned each year
at the start line of the
Boston Marathon.

The surnames of
the two most famous
football commentators in Russia are
Gusev (Goose) and Utkin (Duck).

Before he became a billionaire,
Roman Abramovich ran a
company that made
plastic ducks.

Piggy banks
get their name from
the Old English *pygg*,
meaning 'clay'.

Every new car is
first modelled in clay
by a sculptor.

In 2017,
Bentley launched
a new off-road model
fitted out for falconers,
complete with a perch and
a gauntlet compartment.

Migrating birds
are welcomed to
New Zealand every spring by
the bells of St Paul's, Papanui,
ringing for half an hour.

Birds in cages
hop in the direction
they would migrate,
if they could.

More than half of all
species on Earth are
moving their habitats
due to climate change.

The average frog breeds
eight days earlier than
it would have done
10 years ago.

65 million years ago,
there were frogs that
ate dinosaurs.

Dinosaurs were
living on Earth before
Saturn got its rings.

The world's oldest rock
is 4.38 billion years old.

The world's largest gold nugget
had to be broken up because
it was too big to fit on
the bank's scales.

Only 0.05% of
the Earth's mass
is water.

Glaciers
can move faster
than a speeding train.

Gravity
travels at
the speed of light.

Super Mario's
jumps and falls suggest
he lives on a planet with
eight times more gravity
than Earth.

Jupiter is so close
to its moon Io that it
causes the ground there to
bulge and contract by
hundreds of feet
every day.

Jupiter is
known to have
79 moons.

Pluto's equator
is covered in blades of ice
made of methane.

Not all humans
have methane in
their farts.

Henry II had a court jester
whose Christmas dance featured
a jump, a whistle and a fart.

A *yuleshard*
is someone who is
still preparing for Christmas
on Christmas Eve.

At 3 p.m. on Christmas Eve,
40% of Swedes watch
Donald Duck.

Buying every gift mentioned in
'The Twelve Days of Christmas'
would cost £27,016.92.

Irving Berlin
presented himself with
the Best Original Song Oscar
for 'White Christmas'.

Silent films had
musical accompaniment
to drown out the noise
of the projectors.

Horror films are
the only movie genre
in which more women
appear than men.

The film *Fargo* was
released in Hong Kong as
'Mysterious Murder in Snowy Cream'.

The night-vision camera
released by Sony in 1998
had to be recalled because
it could see through
people's clothes.

The first Sony Walkman
had two headphone jacks
in case it was thought
to be antisocial.

The 2014 version
of the Walkman was sold
inside a bottle of water
to prove it was
waterproof.

Queen Victoria
owned a bulletproof
umbrella.

Canon was
originally spelt 'Kwanon',
after the 1,000-armed Buddhist
goddess of mercy.

Photocopying
was banned in Tibet
in 2010.

The first person
to photocopy a body part
was Andy Warhol.

Wilhelm Röntgen
took the very first X-ray
of his wife Anna Bertha's hand.
Seeing her skeleton made her gasp,
'I have seen my death!'

Dinosaur skeletons
are increasingly bought
by wealthy private collectors,
because museums can't
afford them.

The Kattenkabinet museum
in Amsterdam has works of art by
Rembrandt, Toulouse-Lautrec and
Picasso – but only the ones
featuring cats.

The tagline for the
National Poo Museum
on the Isle of Wight is
'Have You Been?'

Berlin has
a curried-sausage
museum.

The smell of
Play-Doh is
trademarked.

Valium
is present in
potatoes.

Alcohol
is 114 times
as dangerous as
marijuana.

Mighty Morphin Power Rangers
was banned in Malaysia because
Morphin sounded a bit like
'morphine'.

'Groin'
once meant
the snout of a pig.

Dogs inhale
through their nostrils
and exhale through slits on
the sides of their noses.

A poodle–Rottweiler cross is called
a Rottiepoo, a Rottiedoodle
or a Rottweilerpoo.

All Jack Russells
are descended from a dog
called Trump.

Dogs visiting
US National Parks can
be certified as Bark Rangers.

The first public parks
in the US were
cemeteries.

In the 1840s,
Mount Auburn Cemetery
ranked alongside Niagara Falls
as the nation's most popular
tourist attraction.

To tackle the problem of
expanding cemeteries in Brazil,
the mayor of Biritiba-Mirim
suggested that death
be outlawed.

The mayor
of High Wycombe
in Buckinghamshire is
weighed every year to see
if he's got fat during
his term in office.

Plants
make up 82%
of the mass of all
living things.

Only 30%
of Hindus are
vegetarian.

The DNA in your body
could stretch to Pluto
and back again 17 times.

The Sun is
closer to the Earth
during the UK's winter,
not the summer.

In the Qing dynasty,
people swapped their
pillows in the summer
for cooler ceramic ones.

Ancient Greek soldiers
once went on strike
for softer pillows.

The software in
new cars can contain
up to 100 million
lines of code.

The mysterious green code
that begins all the *Matrix* movies
is in fact recipes for sushi.

Matrix
is Latin for
'womb'.

Japan's oldest
porn-movie actress
retired at the
age of 80.

The skull of the
'world's oldest Dutchwoman'
has been carbon dated at
13,000 years old.

5,000 years ago,
the most popular tattoo
was a sheep.

Mentioning
The Girl with the Dragon Tattoo
on your dating profile increases
your replies by one-third.

George V had
a dragon tattoo.

It's illegal in Indiana
to tattoo your eyeballs.

Many Japanese bathhouses
ban people with tattoos.

At Italian swimming pools,
swimming caps are
compulsory.

In French swimming pools,
men are obliged to wear
budgie smugglers.

There's a spa in
the Czech Republic where
you can bathe in beer.

Brno, in the Czech Republic,
has an annual parade of
Silly Walks.

Ráčkovat is
a Czech word meaning
'to mispronounce
your "R"s'.

Bats have
regional accents.

Bats eat
so many insects that
they save US farmers
$22.9 billion a year.

Farm soil quality
can be checked by burying
a pair of underpants and seeing
how long they take
to decompose.

Experts have
warned people not
to boil their underwear
in hotel kettles.

English women
didn't wear underpants
until the 19th century.

In the early 1900s,
women in Chicago could
be fined $50 for wearing
a hatpin over 9 inches long.

The first mass-produced
bicycle for women was called
the Ladies' Psycho.

Penny-farthings
weren't called penny-farthings
until they were almost obsolete.

The Royal Mint made
only seven pennies in 1933:
there were enough in circulation,
but they didn't want to
miss a year.

60% of
1p and 2p coins
are used once, then
put in a jar.

Pickpockets in
17th-century Russia
used sharpened coins
to slice open their
victims' purses.

The Bitcoin network
uses more power than
the whole of Serbia.

The Serbian equivalent of
saying 'Bless you' to a sneeze
is 'Go away, kitten.'

Looking at photos
of puppies and kittens
helps you concentrate.

Paper wasps
know every other wasp
in their colony
by sight.

The record distance
for throwing a paper plane
is 69.14 metres.

Truman Capote
took six paperweights
with him wherever
he went.

The World's Largest Collection of
the World's Smallest Versions
of the World's Largest Things
is based in Kansas.

The world's largest key
collection includes the keys to
the White House toilets,
Mozart's wine cellar
and Hitler's bunker.

The credits for the film *Airplane!*
included Adolf Hitler
as 'Worst Boy'.

Rescuing a damsel
from the train tracks
only ever appeared in films
as a spoof.

Oscars
are not given
for stunts or casting.

The sound
of the doors on the
starship *Enterprise* was made
by pulling a piece of paper
out of an envelope.

The sound at
one Deep Purple concert was
so loud that three people
in the crowd fell
unconscious.

The Welsh mythical hero Culhwch
had a battle cry so loud it
was said to sterilise
women.

Gulf corvina fish
have sex so loudly
they deafen dolphins.

Click beetles can withstand
40 times more G-force
than a fighter pilot.

Montenegro is a
member of NATO but has
no fighter planes.

In Japanese bullfighting,
there are no bullfighters.

The only
ants in Iceland
are in a zoo.

Indigo plants
aren't blue.

Dogs see
in blue and
yellow.

Lizards
in New Guinea
have lime-green blood.

There are over
4,000 pubs in the UK
called the Red Lion.

In 2017,
a pub in Cardiff
apologised to a group of priests
who'd been asked to leave by
staff who assumed they
were on a stag do.

The Popemobile
used by John Paul II on his
visit to Ireland can be rented
out for stag parties.

After the Reformation,
pubs called the Pope's Head
were changed to the King's Head.

King's holly,
a Tasmanian shrub,
is at least 43,000 years old,
but has never been seen to flower.

There is an
eighth continent
called Zealandia,
but 94% of it is
under the sea.

500 times
as much uranium is
dissolved in the sea as
is under the ground.

Plutonium
remains toxic for
at least 100,000 years.

Amazon
owns more than
100,000 robots.

The research that led
to the founding of Google
was funded by grants
from the CIA.

The CIA stages
fake conferences
to lure professors
they want to recruit.

In 2018,
the University of Miami
appointed the US's first
professor of atheism.

The inventor of the bar code
first drew it in sand
on Miami Beach.

In 2013,
a stolen prosthetic arm
was found in a second-hand shop
in Bournemouth.

Mary Shelley is buried
in Bournemouth.

Robert Louis Stevenson wrote
Dr Jekyll and Mr Hyde
in Bournemouth.

Cumberland Clark,
the Bard of Bournemouth,
is widely considered to be
the second-worst poet in
the English language.

The worst pollutant of all
household cleaning products
is air freshener.

Moose Murders,
generally agreed to be
the worst-ever Broadway play,
lasted one night in 1983.

When astronaut Sally Ride
first went into space in 1983,
NASA engineers asked if 100 tampons
would be enough to last her a week.

Elon Musk
works twice as
many hours a week
as the average American.

The risk of
a heart attack
increases by 25%
the Monday after the
clocks go back.

'Widdershins'
is another word for
'anticlockwise'.

In 2017,
the chimes of Big Ben
at Legoland were silenced
to match those of the
real one during its
renovation.

Palm trees
don't have
rings.

Palm oil is
in 50% of all the
products in supermarkets,
from instant noodles
to detergent.

Malaysia
supplies 40% of the
world's palm oil.

The largest hotel
in the world is
in Malaysia.

Hilton Hotels'
largest shareholder
is Chinese.

There is a Belgian hotel
that will rent you a goldfish
to keep you company.

Electric eels
aren't eels.

One way to treat jellyfish stings
is to apply shaving foam and
'shave' the area with
a credit card.

Fish can cough.

Dead Salmon
is a paint colour:
'salmon' is a shade of pink
and 'dead' is a synonym for matt.

Farrow & Ball paint colours include
Savage Ground, Smoked Trout,
Mouse's Back, Mole's Breath,
Setting Plaster, Railings
and Pigeon.

Paint names suggested
by an AI algorithm include
Clardic Fug, Snowbon, Bunflow,
Bank Butt, Caring Tan, Grass Bat,
Stoner Blue, Stanky Bean and Turdly.

Taupe is
the colour of
a French mole.

Naked mole rats have the
same chance of dying
at the age of one
as at 25.

Scientists prepare pet parrots
for their return to life in the wild by
staging parrot murder scenes
and making them watch.

Falcons are
more closely related to parrots
than to hawks or eagles.

There are 550 wild parrots
living in New York City.

Zoologist Francis Buckland
had a parrot that liked to
hail taxis from its perch
by the window.

Hatebeak is
a death-metal band
fronted by a parrot.

The death's head
hawk moth is the only
moth that squeaks
instead of buzzing.

The East African jumping spider
drinks mammals' blood.

Male spiders
in the *Salticidae* family
have fangs longer than
their bodies.

American scientists
have genetically engineered
a 10-legged spider.

Sea urchins
have 10
feet.

In the 1940s,
Americans were
allowed to buy only
three pairs of shoes a year.

Knights Templar
were not allowed to
wear pointy shoes or
speak to women.

The ancient Romans
force-fed snails.

Some Roman statues
had detachable heads
that could be removed if
the person fell from favour.

In 2017,
two 240-year-old letters
were found in Spain inside
the hollow buttocks of a
statue of Jesus.

In 2017,
100,000 euros were found
blocking some toilets
in Geneva.

The world's
most expensive earrings
were sold at auction in Geneva
for $56,290,627.

Cameroon's
president-for-life
spends 15% of his year
in a five-star hotel in Geneva,
where no one knows
what he does.

No one knows
how dinosaurs grew
to be so large.

Quetzalcoatlus
was a feathered dinosaur
as tall as a giraffe that could
fly 10,000 miles non-stop.

Crocodiles in
the prehistoric Sahara
galloped and ate
dinosaurs.

T-Rex had a
top speed of 12 mph
and would have broken
its legs if it had
tried to run.

Woolly mammoths
could be blond, brunette
or ginger.

Jason Allen of Tucson was
invited on *Jimmy Kimmel Live!*
for having the world's
longest leg hair.

To keep the censors happy,
when Elvis went on *The Ed Sullivan Show*,
he was only filmed from
the waist up.

The largest known
anaconda had a
44-inch waist.

There were
473 bananas in
the world's largest
bunch of bananas.

A *pottle* is
a small conical
fruit basket.

To *procaffeinate* is
to put off doing anything until
you've had your first
cup of coffee.

Pecorous means
'full of cows'.

Pullastrine
means 'of, or like,
a pigeon'.

Yawning
is contagious for
budgies.

Orang-utans
blow raspberries
at each other as they
go to sleep.

Growing blackcurrants
was illegal in the US for the
whole of the 20th century.

It's illegal in Canada
to be drunk in charge
of a canoe.

Around 650 AD,
Polynesians in canoes
reached Antarctica.

Antarctica is
the most volcanic region
on Earth.

Antarctic sea spiders
can grow to the size of
dinner plates.

You are advised not to
build snowmen in Antarctica as
it might disturb the animals.

The world's tallest snowwoman
was only 30 feet shorter than
the Statue of Liberty.

In the last 300 years,
there have been only six times
when there's been no snow
on the ground anywhere
in Britain.

Australia has
salt-and-vinegar
flavoured grass.

Atlas,
one of Saturn's moons,
is shaped like a piece
of ravioli.

Genoa airport
has relaxed its rules
on carrying liquids, but
only for pesto.

A single queue at an airport
makes passengers more relaxed
because they don't worry
that other queues are
moving faster.

Useless information
travels faster
than light.

For each
gallon of fuel,
the *QE2* can only travel
the length of a Greyhound bus.

Poodles at
dog shows are
regularly checked
for illegal hairspray.

Most hairspray
isn't vegan.

There's a tanning salon
in St Andrews called
Sun Tan Drews.

There's a tanning salon
in Lytham St Annes called
Lytham St Tanz.

Sunscreen was
invented for people
climbing glaciers.

In 2016,
KFC launched
Extra Crispy Sunscreen,
which smelled like fried chicken.

Airline passengers are
advised to wear sunscreen
by the British Association
of Dermatologists (BAD).

The World Bollard Association
looks after half a billion
bollards.

The roundest
country in the world
is Sierra Leone.

The combined area
of all the parking spaces in
America is larger than Israel,
Cyprus or Macedonia.

US basketball player
Jimmy Butler removed the
rear-view mirrors on his car
as a reminder never
to look back.

In the *Fast and the Furious* movies,
Dwayne 'The Rock' Johnson
drives trucks because
he's too big to fit
into the cars.

'The Rock' was told about
the death of Osama bin Laden
45 minutes before the news media
got hold of the story.

Nick Clegg
announced the news
of the 5p charge on plastic bags
from a notorious Glasgow dogging site.

On 18 April 1930,
the BBC announced that
there was no news that day,
so listeners could enjoy
some piano music.

George Gershwin
learned to play the piano by
copying the movement of the keys
on a friend's pianola.

Anthony Trollope
introduced the postbox
to Britain.

The UK's first postboxes
were painted green to blend in
with the landscape.

During the Second World War,
the tops of British pillar boxes were
coated with special yellow paint
designed to detect poison gas.

Qin Shi Huang,
the first emperor of China,
took mercury pills for immortality
and died of mercury poisoning,
aged 39.

Freddie Mercury
and Michael Jackson began
recording an album together,
but fell out because Jackson kept
bringing his pet llama
to the studio.

Llamas
urinate
backwards.

The ancient Romans
had war dogs that were
trained to fight
in formation.

Sheep fighting is
a popular, but illegal,
sport in Algeria.

Santo Tomás, Peru,
celebrates Christmas by
holding a village punch-up.

A fight broke out after
the first indoor ice-hockey match
between the players and people who
wanted to go skating.

After winning
a fight with a rival,
the male Southeast Asian
mangrove crab does
a victory dance.

The Queen
loves to dance
to 'Dancing Queen'.

When a very large star
quietly turns into a black hole,
it's called a 'massive fail'.

If the Earth had
the density of a black hole,
it would be the size of a peanut.

Alzheimer's patients
lose the ability to smell
peanut butter.

Tortilla chips can
spontaneously
combust.

Australian black kites
collect smouldering sticks
from wildfires and use them
to start new fires to
smoke out prey.

South American scorpions
shed their tails to escape predators,
in the process losing their anus
so they can't poo any more.

Newborn lily beetles
cover themselves in their
parents' excrement so they look
like bird droppings.

In the 19th century,
snake excrement was taken
for lung complaints.

In the 16th century,
women removed body hair
using lotions made of
vinegar and cat poo.

The oldest human hair
was found in a fossilised
hyena turd.

One of the hyenas
in *The Lion King* was
called Shenzi, which means
'worthless bastard'
in Swahili.

Bastardium,
nipponium and pandemonium
are all rejected names for
chemical elements.

The periodic table,
Google and The Beatles' 'Yesterday'
were all conceived
in dreams.

Sleepless in Seattle
T-shirts are a bestseller at
Seattle-Tacoma airport.

The giant armadillo
sleeps for 18.5 hours a day.

Nurse sharks
sleep on the seabed
in piles.

Horses can remember
if you smiled when
they last saw you.

Women have
broader smiles
than men.

There are more
species of ladybirds
than there are species
of mammals.

Only 26 of the 47
British species of ladybird
look like ladybirds.

Ladybirds
recognise each other
by the smell of their feet.

The brains of pigeons have
six times as many nerve cells
as human brains.

Climbing
Mount Everest
causes brain damage.

Nepal has
eight of the 10
highest mountains
in the world.

Mountaineers
can get 'third man syndrome',
where they feel as if someone
else is there with them.

In Madagascar,
every seven years
the bodies of the dead are dug up
to dance with their
living relatives.

Mary Shelley
learned to read
using her mother's
gravestone.

Queen Silvia of Sweden
thinks her palace
is haunted.

A *tommyknocker* is
western American slang
for a ghost that lives
in a mine.

In Texas,
cowboy boots
are tax-exempt.

In a drugs bust
in Detroit in 2017,
undercover agents posing
as dealers attempted to arrest
other undercover agents
posing as buyers.

In 1999,
a man in Connecticut
was barred from joining the police
because his IQ was too high.

In the Philippines,
it's a crime to annoy or
irritate someone.

In Durham in 1350,
William Standupryght
annoyed his neighbours so much
that they all left the village.

In Lincolnshire in 1347,
Letitia Bat was accused
of fornication with
Roger Sweatinbed.

During the Super Bowl,
the two teams produce
11 gallons of sweat
between them.

39% of the
fresh water in the US is
used to cool power stations.

The US uses more electricity for
air-conditioning than the
whole of Africa uses
for everything.

The ash produced by
coal-fired power plants
is more radioactive than
the waste from nuclear
power plants.

A Swedish power plant has
reduced its dependency on coal
by burning clothes from
H&M instead.

The Kentucky
Coal Mining Museum
switched to solar power
in 2017.

Insects are attracted
to solar panels, which they
mistake for water.

Most termites
are blind.

Honeybees
can grasp the
concept of zero.

Chickens
communicate using
over 200 distinct noises.

A *cloop*
is the sound of a cork
being drawn from
the bottle.

A million
plastic bottles
are bought every minute.

7% of the
microplastic in the sea
comes from the paint used for
road markings.

The Japan pig is
a seahorse so tiny
that hundreds of them
would fit into your hand.

In 19th-century Paris,
it was fashionable to take turtles
for walks on a lead.

In 14th-century France,
it was a capital offence to
wear stripes.

In the 1910s,
there was a US baseball team
made up of death-row prisoners,
whose executions were delayed
so long as they kept winning.

Before every
Major League Baseball game,
mud from the Delaware River
is rubbed on the ball.

Punchball is
a sport like baseball
in which you punch the ball
instead of using a bat.

The first punch
Mike Tyson ever threw
was because someone
killed his pigeon.

18th-century actor James Quin
killed a fellow actor in a disagreement
over how to pronounce
the name Cato.

In 1871,
an Ohio lawyer was killed when he
accidentally shot himself demonstrating
how a 'murder victim' might have
accidentally shot himself.

In 1994,
a convicted murderer in England
was given a retrial after it was revealed
that his jurors had consulted
a Ouija board.

In 1474,
a rooster was
put on trial in Switzerland
for laying an egg.

No woman in Britain
has ever been convicted of
stealing a bird's egg.

After the Queen,
the first living person to appear
on a British postage stamp was
Roger Taylor, the drummer
from Queen.

Queen Victoria was given
the first Pekingese dog in Britain.
As he was looted from China,
she named him Looty.

Miniature Pekingese are
also known as Sleeve Pekingese:
they were once kept up the sleeve
for use as weapons.

Of all dog breeds,
Pekingese are the most
genetically similar
to wolves.

Wolves
are more intelligent
than dogs.

Artificial intelligence
can beat 99% of humans at
Fantasy Football.

Two tech billionaires
who think we live in a
computer simulation have
hired a team to work on
how to break out of it.

Disney has
filed a patent for
huggable robots.

The surname Disney
was originally D'Isney and
meant someone who came from
Isigny in Normandy.

Yen Sid,
the sorcerer in *Fantasia*,
is 'Disney' backwards.

Kiss
is Swedish
for 'pee'.

The longest
penis on record is
only three inches shorter
than the shortest
man on record.

Mambo is Swedish for
an adult who still lives with
their parents.

Fremdscham is
German for being embarrassed
for someone else.

An *attaccabottoni*
is Italian for someone
who only talks about themself.

Egduutei
is Mongolian for
the irresistible urge
to pinch or squeeze
something or someone
unbearably cute.

Stockholm trains
named by schoolchildren
include Best Friend, Glitter, and
The Kisses and Hugs Train.

To become
someone's best friend
takes 200 hours.

Only death
releases someone
from the Official Secrets Act.

Shakespeare killed
two of his characters
by baking them into a pie.

A Bedfordshire Clanger
was a long pie with
meat at one end
and pudding
at the other.

The annual Wigan pie-eating contest
was scandalised in 2005, when
it was found that the pies
were imported from
nearby Bolton.

Italy holds
an annual Hide-and-Seek
world championship.

America has a
National Grocery Bag Packing
competition.

The only member of the
Ecuadorean Olympic ski team
trains on tarmac using
roller skis.

Roller-skating messengers
were once used for the
17 miles of corridors
in the Pentagon.

The most decorated
US marine in history
was called Chesty Puller.

1 in 4 Americans
don't know which country
the US declared independence from.

Japan
has a school where
pupils learn to behave like
Anne of Green Gables.

When Greenland left the EEC,
the community's area
was reduced
by half.

If the San Francisco Bay Area
were a country, it would have
the 16th largest GDP
in the world.

10% of
the GDP of Tuvalu
comes from the registration of
.tv domain names.

The French TV
version of *Bake Off*
uses music from
Doctor Who.

In the 2009 Eurovision Song Contest,
43 Azerbaijanis voted for Armenia,
some of whom were later
interviewed by
the police.

Under Section 54 of the
Metropolitan Police Act 1839,
it's illegal to carry a plank
along the pavement.

'Plankton' and
'planet' both come from
the same Greek word meaning
'to wander about'.

A passenger aircraft
without windows would
be 50% lighter.

56% of France's
military aircraft
are unfit to fly.

In 2006,
the nuclear-powered aircraft carrier
USS *Ronald Reagan* was
incapacitated by a
jellyfish attack.

Nomura's jellyfish
can weigh up to
440 pounds.

A Danish scientist
has invented
jellyfish
crisps.

Wolves returned
to Denmark in 2017
for the first time
in 200 years.

In 2017,
deer were seen
eating a human body
for the first time.

The first shark attack
recorded in British waters
took place in 2017 and
left its victim with a
cut on his thumb.

The minute leaf chameleon
is the size of a human
thumbnail.

The cucamelon
is the size of a grape,
but looks like a watermelon
and tastes like cucumber.

Half the world's
legal cannabis is grown
by the Chinese.

Until 1916,
Harrods sold
heroin and cocaine.

Queen Victoria
took cocaine with
Winston Churchill.

Slang terms
for heroin include
'dog food', 'elephant',
'witch', 'horsebite'
and 'gravy'.

Colonel Sanders
was sued by KFC for saying
their gravy was 'sludge' and
'wallpaper-paste like'.

The South Korean
Ministry of Food and Drug Safety
has warned people not to
add wasps to cocktails.

Bees' tongues
have no taste buds.

The 'oral size illusion'
is when your tongue gives
you the impression that
a hole is bigger
than it is.

The heat of the
hole that the egg of
a Pacific green sea turtle
is incubated in
determines
its sex.

'Turtle rabbit'
is the literal translation
of the Aztec for
'armadillo'.

A rabbit's nose
can twitch more than
120 times a minute.

A *nasothek*
is a collection
of nose sculptures.

In ancient Rome,
being born with a crooked nose
was a sign of leadership.

Your nose is
always in your eyeline,
but your brain has learned
to ignore it.

The word 'sneeze'
was originally 'neeze'.
Nobody knows where
the 's' came from.

Nobody knows
whether or not
bats fart.

Cats
could follow
human instructions
if they wanted to,
but they don't.

In 1963,
a Parisian stray
called Félicette became
the first cat sent into space.

From space, you can tell
East Berlin from West Berlin
because streetlights in the East
use yellow sodium vapour,
while those in the West
are fluorescent white.

The 1936 Berlin Olympics
were sponsored by
Coca-Cola.

Russia's
October Revolution
is celebrated in
November.

July
used to rhyme
with 'truly'.

The most popular
pub-quiz team name in Britain
is QuizTeam Aguilera.

Christina Ricci
has an irrational fear
of houseplants.

40% of Americans
say they are too scared
to ask what is in
their hotdogs.

Fear
is good for
stock markets.

When chased by lions,
zebras fart loudly
with every stride.

Zebra crossings
can cause epileptic fits
and migraines.

The NHS uses
more than 10% of the
world's pagers.

Anaesthetics
work on plants.

In the Middle Ages,
peonies were used
to treat lunacy.

Plants can be
trained to expect
rewards.

Sniffer dogs can be
trained to detect
works of art.

Paintings
that don't fit into lifts
are less popular
at auctions.

The Swedish
for 'lift' is
hiss.

The Irish
for 'escalator'
is *staighre beo*,
'living stairs'.

12,000
Americans die
falling down stairs
each year.

Unmarried people are more likely to
fall down stairs than married people,
and previously married people
more likely to do so
than either.

The world record for
the most stairs climbed
while balancing another
person upside down
on one's head
is 90.

Guinness has world records for
'Most Mousetraps Released
on the Tongue' and 'Most
Fan Blades Stopped
by the Tongue'.

A pangolin's tongue
is longer than
its body.

Possession
of a pangolin
is illegal in Ghana.

It's illegal
in 18 US states to
sell fake urine.

In New Zealand,
imperial measures are illegal,
apart from pints of beer,
which are regarded
as a description,
not a measure.

In Britain in the First World War,
it was illegal to serve someone
more beer than they asked for.

In London in 1814,
eight people drowned
when a vat in a brewery ruptured,
creating a 15-foot tidal wave of beer.

The Guinness brewery
is 259 years into its
9,000-year lease.

Lagar is Irish for
'weakness' or 'depression',
and *lágar* means 'beer'.

Seelenklempner,
the German for 'psychiatrist',
literally translates as
'soul plumber'.

The 93rd-most-cited psychologist
of the 20th century was
Edwin Boring.

The shortest published scientific paper,
'An Unsuccessful Self-Treatment
of a Case of "Writer's Block"',
contains no words.

Mark Twain's uncensored autobiography,
published 100 years after his death,
made him a bestselling author in
the 19th, 20th and 21st centuries.

The expressions
'PIN number' and 'ATM machine' are
examples of Redundant Acronym
Syndrome syndrome.

A 'murdermonger' is
a writer of murder mysteries.

Sea lions
are more murderous
than actual lions.

In the last 30,000 years,
the Great Barrier Reef
has died five times.

Sugar
heals infections
that even antibiotics
can't cure.

Kierkegaard
made coffee by
filling a cup with sugar,
pouring in coffee until
it dissolved and then
downing the lot.

The dome of the Taj Mahal
is held together with
sugar, fruit juice
and egg whites.

In 17th-century India,
smoothies were made by
shaking mangoes till they liquefied,
then sucking the juice out
through a hole.

The shape of Perrier bottles
is based on that of
Indian clubs.

In the US,
bottled water
outsells all other
soft drinks combined.

The entire water supply
of Bermuda comes from
rain collected by
special roofs.

85% of bikinis
never get
wet.

German physicist Theodor Kaluza
taught himself to swim
from a book.

Pigeons
can be taught
to recognise words.

Reuters started as
a flock of pigeons ferrying
financial news between Germany
and Belgium.

In 2018,
news of forest fires in Canada
caused panic buying
of toilet paper
in Taiwan.

In 2014,
protesters in Moscow
were arrested for holding
invisible posters.

Researchers in China
have invented printable
invisible ink.

1 in 6 Georgians
mistakenly think their country
is a member of the EU.

One-third of
all flight delays
in Europe are caused by
French air traffic controllers.

To avoid confusion,
African reed frogs
change colour
during orgies.

Sex between
two hummingbirds
lasts three to five
seconds.

Graham crackers
were originally intended
to reduce people's
sexual urges.

Eating nuts
improves sperm count.

Fox squirrels
arrange their nuts
by variety.

The 40 squirrels
that appear in one scene in
Charlie and the Chocolate Factory
spent 10 months in training.

Director David Fincher
had a stuntman fall down stairs
12 times for one scene in *Fight Club*,
and then used the first take.

The word 'slapstick'
comes from a stick used in
16th-century Italian comedy to
make a slapping noise without
hurting another actor.

Billiards was once played with 'maces',
or sticks with blocks on one end.
Cues developed from players
getting better scores by
using the 'wrong'
end of the stick.

Billiards was the first sport
to have a world championship.

In 1863,
a hot-air balloon
equipped with a billiard table,
a photographic workshop, a lavatory
and a refreshment room successfully
flew 400 miles.

The Church of the
Flying Spaghetti Monster is
banned from advertising
in Germany.

In Brooklyn,
you can enjoy
spaghetti Bolognese
doughnuts.

Slouching
can help you solve
maths problems.

Pilates
was devised
as a way to keep
prisoners-of-war fit.

Most yoga poses
date back only
150 years.

Until the 1970s,
almost no women
ate their own placenta.

Genetically speaking,
placentas belong to the baby,
not the mother.

Debussy's father
owned a china shop.

In 2013,
a Chinese father
hired virtual hitmen to
kill his son's character in
the computer game he played
so he would focus on getting a job.

Japanese employees
can hire someone else to
get told off by the boss.

Russians can hire a private jet
to take Instagram pictures in,
but it never takes off.

The downdraught
from the helicopter
filming the mountain scene
at the start of *The Sound of Music*
knocked Julie Andrews over
after each take.

Helicopters can protect crops
from frost by flying over them
and moving the air around.

Apple consumption in the US
tripled in the 10 years after
McDonald's added
sliced apples to
their menu.

The consumption of gin in
18th-century England was
25 times higher than it is today.

The quinine
in tonic water
glows a brilliant blue
under UV light.

People
in Iceland can be
stopped by the police for
driving under the influence
of the Northern Lights.

Driving a car
for 12 miles has the
same carbon footprint as
one 'all-day breakfast' sandwich.

More people in Britain
work in the sandwich industry
than in agriculture.

Italians
use '*al fresco*'
to mean 'in prison',
like the US slang
'in the cooler'.

In 2017,
eight donkeys in India
spent four days in prison for
eating valuable plants.

Tomato plants
release chemicals that
turn caterpillars
into cannibals.

Caterpillars are
more likely to vomit
when on their own.

Bats
swim using
the butterfly stroke.

The longest-ever kayak trip
was completed by a man
who couldn't swim.

J. K. Rowling
couldn't submit her
final changes to *The Casual Vacancy*
because an aardvark had chewed
through a power cable.

The second Harry Potter film
came with a warning that it contained
'mild language and horror, and
fantasy spiders'.

Spiders of the *Selenops* family
can spin around eight times
in a second.

All galaxies,
regardless of size,
rotate once every
billion years.

There are
galaxies called the
Cartwheel, the Tadpole,
the Cigar, the Sunflower
and the Sombrero.

Cashpoint, Bubble Wrap, Jet Ski,
Ping Pong and Memory Stick
are all brand names.

In 2017,
a peacock caused £3,000 worth
of damage to a new Range Rover after
seeing its reflection in the paintwork
and mistaking it for a rival.

In 2018,
an emotional support peacock
named Dexter was denied access to
an American Airlines flight, despite
having a ticket and his own seat.

There is no evidence that
peahens choose their partner
because of his plumage.

Peacock spider species
include *Skeletorus* and
Sparklemuffin.

Some wasps
cover their partner's eyes
when mating.

Wasps can be deterred
by hanging up a paper bag,
which they mistake for
an enemy nest.

A Venus flytrap
can take over a week
to digest a large insect
and spit out its bones.

Venus has
a crater named
Mulan.

The Earth
hums.

A special tartan
has been designed
for exploring
Mars.

In medieval Scotland,
the national drink
was claret.

Pershittie is
a 19th-century Scots word
meaning 'hard to please'.

Sir Walter Scott's novel
Anne of Geierstein, in which a woman
is cursed by an opal, caused
opal sales in Europe
to drop by 50%.

The first work of fiction
about travelling back in time
to kill the young Adolf Hitler
was published in 1941.

The Vatican's chief astronomer
has written a book called
*Would You Baptise an
Extraterrestrial?*

In 2017,
the Vatican banned the use
of gluten-free bread for
Holy Communion.

In 320 AD,
the Catholic Church
made it a sin to eat
sausages.

In 17th-century Japan,
people put chillies in their socks
to keep their toes warm.

Sprinkling black pepper
into a load of laundry
will stop it fading.

Red, green and yellow peppers
are all from the same plant but
in various stages of ripeness.

Birds can't
taste chilli.

Crows
can count
up to six.

Counting sheep
to try to get to sleep
keeps you awake
for longer.

'Sheep-stealing' is
the practice of one American church
luring the congregation
of another.

Sheep smuggling
used to be called
'owling'.

In 2012,
thieves in the Czech Republic
stole an entire
ski lift.

Stonehenge
was built by
the Welsh.

China's
Tomb-Sweeping Day
is for tending your relatives' graves
and for young couples to
have their first date.

Oil Nationalisation Day
is a public holiday
in Iran.

In Bermuda,
the nearest weekday to 24 May is
the first day of the year when
Bermuda shorts may be
worn as formal wear.

On formal occasions,
Barack Obama wore the same
dinner jacket and shoes for
all eight years of
his presidency.

The Simpsons predicted
Donald Trump would become president
16 years before he was elected.

Calvin Coolidge
chose all his children's clothes
and insisted his sons wore
tuxedos at dinner.

Calvin Klein
kept a Pantone card
in his kitchen so his chef could
get the colour of his coffee
exactly right.

Pantone
created a new shade of purple
in honour of Prince called
Love Symbol #2.

Prince's
favourite colour
was orange.

Victor Hugo
could fit a whole orange
in his mouth.

At the age of 69,
Victor Hugo had sex with
40 different people
in five months.

Male brown widow spiders
prefer to mate with older females,
even though they are more likely
to be eaten by them afterwards.

Squid change sexual position
when requested to do so
by their partners.

In 2017,
underperforming employees
at a Manchester call centre were
punished by having a dead squid
dropped on their faces.

The Nazca people
employed someone
to walk around with a
dead fox on their head.

The first Western eyewitness account
of India described it as having
ants the size of foxes.

Mosquitoes on the
London Underground's Piccadilly Line
are genetically different from
those on the Bakerloo Line.

Baker Island,
in the middle of the Pacific,
is the last place on Earth
to ring in the new year.

The world's
smallest flightless bird is the
Inaccessible Island
rail.

Cleaning a train
in Pakistan takes
40 people four hours.

Human nose grease
can be used to clean
photographic
negatives.

People enjoy their food more
if they share photographs
of it on social media.

The customer
who ordered the
world's smallest sushi,
made with a single grain of rice,
was so moved she cried for
an hour and a half.

Rui-katsu ('tear-seeking')
is a Japanese therapy in which
women pay to have a good cry
with a handsome man.

Three Argentinian rugby players
use their new tooth implants
as bottle openers.

When the Chinese
invented the compass,
they used it for
fortune-telling.

Whenever
a hurricane is forecast,
sales of strawberry Pop-Tarts
increase sevenfold.

Poppies were
first used as a symbol of
the Napoleonic Wars.

There is a new
genetically engineered poppy
whose seeds won't make you
fail a drugs test.

Elvis Presley
wanted to be a federal
drug enforcement agent and
was given a specially made badge
by President Nixon.

President Calvin Coolidge
enjoyed buzzing for his staff
and hiding under the Oval Office desk
while they searched for him.

President Lyndon B. Johnson
had an amphibious car that he liked
to drive into the water, shouting,
'The brakes don't work,
we're going under!'

18 former presidents
of Switzerland
are still alive.

People with
Cotard's syndrome
believe themselves
to be dead.

A lifetime's association of
certain letters with specific colours
can be caused by early exposure
to Fisher-Price fridge magnets.

The world's
most advanced magnet is
called 'the double pancake' and
weighs as much as a Boeing 747.

In 1935,
Vogue readers
were told that pancakes
'are not worth eating
unless paper thin'.

The British
overcook roast beef
by an average of
41 minutes.

Jamie Oliver has
a customised Land Rover that
slow-roasts meat under the bonnet
and makes butter and ice cream
in the wheel drums.

Chopsticks
were designed to be
used for cooking,
not eating.

Chicken noodle soup
really does relieve symptoms
of the common cold.

The US Centers for
Disease Control and Prevention
have a 'Most Wanted' list
for flu viruses.

It's illegal to
get into a black London taxi
if suffering from food poisoning,
anthrax, measles or leprosy.

Vivaldi
suffered from
asthma.

25% of Americans
who catch salmonella
from pet chickens admit
to having kissed them recently.

Prairie dogs
greet each other
with kisses.

In 2015,
a woman in Indiana
was shot in the foot by
her dog, Trigger.

The inventor of
the Uzi sub-machine gun
was imprisoned for illegal
possession of a firearm.

The Apple III computer
was built without a cooling fan
because Steve Jobs hated
the noise.

Joe Davis won the
1933 World Snooker Championship
in a building named
after himself.

The only basketball coach at
Kansas University with a losing record
was James Naismith, the man who
invented basketball.

From 1541 to 1555,
playing bowls was illegal
for commoners, except on
Christmas Day.

25% of the
world's prisoners
are in the US.

When Oscar Wilde was in prison,
he had special dispensation to
have his light on at night
so he could keep reading.

A restaurant in Connecticut
gives diners a free book
with their meal.

Timothy Dexter wrote a book
with no punctuation, but included
a sheet of punctuation marks for
the reader to distribute
as they pleased.

The exclamation mark
was originally called the
'point of admiration'.

In Egypt's Middle Kingdom,
it was a mark of high status
to have a folding stool.

In the Cabinet Office
at No. 10 Downing Street,
the prime minister's chair is the
only one with arms.

A Dutch designer
has invented a chair that
gives an electric shock to people
who say 'Yes, but . . .' in meetings.

Researchers in Singapore
have built a robot that
can assemble an
IKEA chair.

Nintendo
is Japanese for
'leave luck to Heaven'.

According to Nintendo,
Mario isn't a plumber.

In 2018,
a plane full of
Norwegian plumbers
had to turn back because
of a broken toilet.

In 2009,
a British Airways plane
was delayed from taking off
for half an hour because it
didn't have an ashtray
in the lavatory.

In 2015,
a Southampton to Dublin flight
had to turn back after a bee got stuck
in the flight instruments.
It was a Flybe flight.

In 1952,
a US Air Force lieutenant
accidentally shot down
his own plane.

In 1943,
a US destroyer
accidentally torpedoed
a ship that was carrying
President Roosevelt.

The US Navy uses
Xbox controllers to
operate periscopes.

The US director of the
International Knife Throwers
Hall of Fame is called
Jack Dagger.

Winston Churchill
trained his pet budgie to walk
up and down his dining-room table
carrying a salt spoon.

When Danish explorer
Peter Freuchen was buried
by an avalanche at the North Pole,
he hacked his way out with a tool
made of his own frozen poo.

A butcher in Totnes
who got trapped in his freezer in 2018
had to batter his way out with
a frozen black pudding.

The French
don't have Christmas pudding
or Christmas crackers
at Christmas.

The pioneers of the
French naturist movement
were a married couple
called Lecoq.

Louis XVI
issued a decree
prohibiting anyone from carrying
a handkerchief larger than his.

Lawn,
a fine cloth used
to make handkerchiefs,
gets its name from the
French city of Laon.

The curator of the
British Lawnmower Museum
is allergic to grass.

As a child,
Welsh jockey Sean Bowen
was allergic to horses
and practised riding
by sitting on the
arm of a sofa.

US ice-hockey goalie
Chris Truehl is
allergic to ice.

Under a US law
signed by Ronald Reagan,
July is National Ice Cream Month
and 15 July is National
Ice Cream Day.

February
was known to the
Anglo-Saxons as *Solmoneth,*
or 'mud month'.

Over 100 men a month
visit a hospital in Bangkok to
have their penis whitened.

The inventor of the bra
had a pet whippet
called Clytoris.

Abraham Lincoln
patented an inflatable ship.

In 2017,
China imported
33 shipping containers
of avocados – up from
zero in 2014.

The flag of the Philippines has
the blue stripe on top in peacetime
and the red stripe on top
in wartime.

The first red flag
symbolising workers' rights
was dyed with
calf's blood.

Blood donors
in Sweden are sent
a thank-you text message
when their blood gets used.

The first Kleenex tissues were
made from the same material as
the gas-mask filters during
the First World War.

During the Second World War,
the Northern Ireland Assembly building
was covered in cow manure
to camouflage it.

Defecating
causes sloths
as much pain as
childbirth.

The oldest human
settlement in Australia
was found by a man looking
for a lavatory.

Australians feel they need to earn
more than three times as much
as people in the Caribbean
to be equally happy.

Warriors in
Papua New Guinea made
daggers from their enemies'
thigh bones.

Fractures
can be diagnosed by
holding a tuning fork to the bone:
if it rings like a bell,
all's well.

The Japanese have
invented a noise-cancelling fork
to counteract the sound of people
slurping their noodles.

In 2018,
the Thai prime minister
directed reporters' questions
to a cardboard cut-out
of himself.

Sarcasm
is banned
in North Korea.

70% of
South Koreans
aged under 30 are
short-sighted.

South Korean women
who wear glasses to work
are seen as unprofessional.

A *zoilist* is someone
who gets pleasure from
finding fault.

A *cumberground* is someone
whose only purpose is
to take up space.

Whipper-tooties are
feeble excuses for not
doing something.

Crytoscopophilia
is the urge to look through
the windows of someone's house
as you pass by.

In France,
you can ask the postie
to look in on your
elderly parents.

For its first 300 years,
the word 'worrying' was
what dogs did to sheep.

For its first 100 years,
the word 'mugger' meant
someone who sold mugs.

600 billion
cups of coffee are
drunk each year.

You are 10 million times
more likely to be struck by
lightning than hit by a piece
of falling space debris.

The pressure
inside a proton is
a billion billion billion times
greater than that at the bottom
of the Mariana Trench.

The scientific journal
Academic Emergency Medicine
records an experiment in which
sheep were tasered while
high on crystal meth.

Over 15,000 published
scientific studies mention
Arnold Schwarzenegger.

William Shatner
had a kidney stone removed
and sold it for
$25,000.

Some people
can produce
goosebumps
on demand.

7% of Americans
have bashful bladder syndrome,
which means they can't pee
if they can see or hear
another person.

80% of women
hover over public toilets.

Bacteria can
penetrate six layers
of loo paper.

Rats can
tread water for
three days and
survive being flushed
down the lavatory.

Funnel-web spiders
can live in water
for 30 hours.

Coconut crabs
grow as big
as dogs.

A blind man who is
scared of dogs has been
given the UK's first
guide horse.

The *Titanic*'s gym
had an electric horse
for passengers to hone
their riding skills.

President Ulysses S. Grant
was arrested for
speeding on
a horse.

Horses
have three more
facial expressions than
chimpanzees.

Chimpanzees
can be taught to play
Rock, Paper, Scissors.

60% of primatologists have
been scratched by a primate,
and 40% have been
bitten by one.

Pottos are
primates that smell
like curry.

75 million bacteria
per square centimetre
can live in one rubber duck.

Ducks' penises
grow and shrink
with the seasons.

Summer and autumn
are the times when
Google searches
for 'hair loss'
peak.

Pulling someone's hair is a
legal tackle in American football:
if it reaches to their jersey,
it counts as part of
their uniform.

To catch cheating footballers,
scientists have invented
anti-diving shin pads.

The backs
of playing cards
used to be left blank so
people could make
notes on them.

The translator of
Finnegans Wake into Chinese
is having to write footnotes
for 80% of the words.

Detective Speechley
is a spokesman
for the NYPD.

Stephen Hawking wrote
'Galeelaeo' and 'Ahristottal' in his
lecture notes so his speech machine
would pronounce them properly.

The ancient Greeks
had a contraceptive suppository
made of frankincense, myrrh
and blister beetles.

A panda's sperm count
is a hundred times higher
than a man's.

Pandas
can distinguish
18 shades of grey.

Pandas
are losing their
black eye patches,
and no one knows why.

No one knows why
the upside-down catfish
swims upside down.

Goldfish can
survive for five months
without oxygen.

Praying mantises are
the only insects known
to see in 3D.

Insect burgers
are available in
Switzerland.

Yellville, Arkansas,
celebrates Thanksgiving
by dropping turkeys from
a light aircraft.

In 1605,
an Act of Parliament
made the celebration
of Bonfire Night
compulsory.

During the Second World War,
paraffin was used
to make cakes.

France and
French Polynesia
have special mailboxes for
baguette deliveries.

French became
the official language
of the Aosta Valley in Italy
three years before it
was adopted by
France itself.

Drunken fights among
pétanque players are known
in the French press as
bouliganism.

France
has a population of
wild hamsters.

A group of pheasants
is called a 'bouquet'.

Ptarmigan
is eaten by 8%
of Icelanders at
Christmas.

The past tense of 'snow'
used to be 'snew'.

Snow fleas
survive the cold because
their bodies contain
natural antifreeze.

It is only safe
to eat snow that has
fallen within the
last half-day.

According to the
Office for National Statistics,
Britons eat 50% more than
they say they do.

The Welsh
for 'peaches'
literally translates as
'woolly plums'.

In the 17th century,
potatoes were cut into
fishy shapes and fried as a fish
substitute when it was too
cold to go fishing.

People with
auto-brewery syndrome
can get drunk from
eating chips.

Pancakes
in food ads are
drizzled with motor oil
because it looks better
than maple syrup.

The director of Canada's
Avian Science and Conservation Centre
is called Professor Bird.

Birds have a
built-in 'smell map'
that helps them navigate
featureless oceans.

A pelican's bill
can hold as much water as
two flushes of a toilet.

50 geese
can produce
5,000 pounds of
excrement a year.

The UK has
more Wildlife Trust
nature reserves than
branches of McDonald's.

Donald Trump
asked the White House chef
to recreate items from the
McDonald's menu for him.

When Donald Trump
asked the Guggenheim Museum
to lend the White House a Van Gogh,
they offered him a solid gold
toilet instead.

To *quomodocunquize*
is to make money in
any way possible.

A *lanspresado* is
a 17th-century word for
the friend who never seems to
have any money with them.

A *tunklehead* is
Maine slang for
an 'idiot'.

Euneirophrenia
is the peaceful feeling
experienced on emerging
from a nice dream.

Birds sing
in their dreams.

Dogs only make
sad faces if there's a
person watching.

A complete set of
two-inch-square cotton
Pantone colour swatches
costs $7,395.

Pope Francis's watch
cost less than a
paperback
Bible.

Pope Benedict XVI
commissioned a special
eau de cologne for himself
that smelled like the
Grotto at Lourdes.

Modern Catholic exorcisms
are carried out by reciting
Latin prayers over
a mobile phone.

After the Gunpowder Plot,
English Catholics were banned from
voting, practising law or serving as
officers in the army or navy
until 1829.

The word 'conspire'
comes from the Latin *conspirare*,
meaning 'to breathe together'.

Hvalreki is
Icelandic for 'windfall'
and 'beached whale'.

The Latin for 'pan pipes'
was the same as the word
for a whale's blowhole.

Bowhead whales
rub up against rocks to
exfoliate their skin.

Sea urchins can
drill holes in solid rock
with their teeth.

10% of chipped teeth
are caused by popcorn.

Over 25% of the
mentions of teeth in
the Bible involve
'gnashing'.

Tasleek is a Saudi word
meaning to nod along and
pretend to care what the
other person is saying.

In 19th-century France,
the least-important dinner guests
sat at the ends of the table.
Honoured guests were
seated in the middle,
with more people
to talk to.

People
walk faster when
passing banks.

On the Moon,
skipping is more efficient
than walking.

The grunts of a tennis player
become higher-pitched
when they're losing.

Venus Williams has spent
more than a year of her life
at Wimbledon.

Novak Djokovic
never uses the same shower
twice in a row.

Canadian
snooker player
'Big Bill' Werbeniuk
drank eight pints of beer
before a match, then one
for each frame.

In the 19th century,
a 'pool room' was where
people placed bets on
horse racing.

Pool started as a
medieval game called
jeu de la poule, in which you
threw rocks at a chicken.

Pet chickens
in Silicon Valley have
their own personal chefs.

The 17th-century game
Sparrow Mumbling involved
holding a live bird
in your mouth.

Robins
go through puberty
every year.

If your metabolism was
as fast as a hummingbird's,
you would need to drink
a can of Coke a minute
just to stay alive.

Hummingbirds' hearts
beat 10 times a second
and are the size of
the rubber on the
end of a pencil.

From the 16th to the 19th century,
England had a world monopoly
on pencil production.

You can win
a game of Monopoly
after only four turns.

Vikings were
buried with board games
to combat boredom
in the afterlife.

There are more people today
pretending to be Vikings in the
computer game *Vikings: War of Clans*
than there ever were actual Vikings.

In Welsh mythology,
fairies ride corgis
into battle.

In Norse mythology,
Naglfar was a ship made from
the untrimmed fingernails
of the dead.

The longest human thumbnail
ever recorded measures
six and a half feet.

The world's largest cruise ship
is five times the size
of the *Titanic*.

Lightning storms
are twice as likely in
shipping lanes as in the
rest of the ocean.

A 'dirty' thunderstorm
is when lightning is produced
in a volcanic plume.

The number of people
killed by lightning today
is a tenth of what
it was in the
1940s.

Only 139 cars
were produced in the US
during the Second World War.

In 1820s Manhattan,
there was one pig for
every five humans.

In 1899,
Henry Bliss became
the first American pedestrian
to be killed by a car.

The man who invented
one-way streets, roundabouts,
taxi stands and stop signs
never learned to drive.

French people
are 19 times less likely
to wait for the green man
than Japanese people.

Hitchhikers in Sweden
wait longest for a ride;
those in Iraq wait
shortest.

According to
research by North Korea,
the world's second-happiest country
is North Korea.

The demilitarised zone
between North and South Korea is
home to 5,097 different species.

Insects make up
72% of all animals, but only
2% of endangered species.

Until the 19th century,
Primrose Hill in London
was inhabited
by wolves.

New York City controls its
rat problem by giving them
the menopause.

In 1902,
after the French
colonial government in Hanoi
offered one cent for every rat's tail,
enterprising Vietnamese started
rat farms to earn the bounty.

In 1959,
the US government
issued a memo saying that
yetis could only be killed
in self-defence.

Sloths can
hold their breath
for 40 minutes.

Ostriches
have four kneecaps.

Babies' kneecaps
don't show up
on X-rays.

Babies born into
the Budweiser family have
five drops of Budweiser dropped
on their tongues as a first taste.

Beer
is more nutritious
than bread.

The world record for
the most beer mats flipped
and caught with the same hand
is held by a man called
Matt Hand.

'As much food as one's hand can hold'
was Dr Johnson's *Dictionary*'s
definition of 'lunch'.

The bowl
formed by cupping
one's hands together is
called a *'gowpen'*.

Rachmaninov
had enormous hands:
he could span 12 piano keys
with either one.

Jimi Hendrix's
father told him his
left-handedness meant
he was born of
the Devil.

The Jim Smith Society has
over 2,000 members worldwide,
all called Jim Smith.

The Royal Society for the
Protection of Birds was founded in 1889
by women denied membership of the
British Ornithologists' Union.

Beyoncé's
fans are called
the Beyhive.

The WD-40 fan club
has over 100,000 members.

J. R. R. Tolkien
described his fans
as 'deplorable'.

1 in every 160
New Zealanders was
involved in the production of
The Lord of the Rings.

Jurassic Park was
hit by the most powerful
hurricane ever to reach Hawaii,
but Richard Attenborough
slept right through it.

In the movie *Chinese Zodiac*,
Jackie Chan had 15 credits, including
actor, writer, director, composer
and catering coordinator.

Amber Rudd
was credited as
'aristocracy coordinator'
on *Four Weddings and a Funeral.*

A. A. Milne
planned a film adaptation
of *Pride and Prejudice*,
with Mr Darcy played
by Eeyore.

5% of piglets
are crushed to death by
their own mothers.

The world record for
crushing concrete blocks
with the head is held by
a 17-year-old boy
from Bosnia.

Concrete
cannot be recycled.

The average lifespan
of a skyscraper
is 42 years.

The useful lifespan
of a coffee stirrer
is four seconds.

The longest-living animal
is the red sea urchin,
which survives for
up to 200 years
in the wild.

Brandt's bat is
the longest-living bat:
it can live for 40 years
and weighs as much
as eight paperclips.

Paperclips
float on water.

The world's biggest paperclip
is 30 feet long and
nine feet wide.

You can buy a
Prada paperclip
for $185.

The Ritz-Carlton hotel in
Riyadh has been converted
into the world's most
luxurious prison.

Cellblocks is
a cryptocurrency
used in American prisons.

Cryptocurrency
worth $534 million
was stolen in Japan in 2018,
making it the biggest theft in
the history of the world.

In 2005,
security guards at
Australia's parliament were
banned from calling MPs 'mate'.
The ban was lifted within 24 hours
for being un-Australian.

There are two places
in Australia called
Dismal Swamp.

Trees sweat
to cool down.

By using bidets
instead of toilet paper,
Americans could save
15 million trees a year.

Woodpeckers bang
their heads into trees
at 15 miles an hour,
12,000 times a day.

The Canary Islands
have dandelion
trees.

75% of the sesame seeds
grown in Mexico are used on
McDonald's burger buns.

Until the 1870s,
all Camembert was made
by a single family.

Since the 1970s,
France has lost
50 types of
cheese.

The world's most
expensive cheese is
made from donkey's milk.

Thomas Hardy's novels
were considered so disgusting
they were sold in plain,
brown wrappers.

Thomas Hardy, Rudyard Kipling
and Joseph Conrad all wrote books
the size of postage stamps for
Queen Mary's doll's house.

Christina Foyle,
owner of Foyle's bookshop,
read an entire book every day,
never did her own housework
and only drank champagne.

There's an orchid
in Madagascar that
smells like champagne.

There's a secret pub
inside the Tower of London
that only Beefeaters and
their guests can visit.

In 18th-century London,
a sick person could pay
three guineas to bathe
in beef soup.

The average Briton
eats 17.3 kg of beef a year.

Dung beetles
contain more protein
than beef does.

80% of Japan's protein
comes from the sea.

The plastic waste that
goes into the oceans every year
is enough to fill five shopping bags
for every foot of shoreline
in the world.

Half of all the plastic
that has ever existed
was made in the
last 13 years.

When Jung and Freud first met,
their conversation
lasted 13 hours.

Sheep can
recognise celebrities
with 80% accuracy.

Elmo is
the only non-human to
testify before the
US Congress.

Bert and Ernie
only have one eyebrow
between them.

DVDs of the
first few series
of *Sesame Street* are
labelled 'Adult Only'.

By the standards of the
rest of the animal kingdom,
human beings should be 200 times
as murderous as they are.

The longest
New York City has gone
without a murder
is 12 days.

A Chewbacca defence
is a lawyer's way of confusing
the other side by spouting
irrelevant nonsense.

Chewbacca is 7' 6",
the same height as the
tallest high-school basketball
player in the world.

The largest snowflake
ever recorded was
15 inches across.

The longest and shortest
pub names in Britain are both
in Stalybridge, Manchester.

Manchester United MacGyver
is a 19-year-old Namibian
footballer.

Joey Barton
missed his planned debut
for Manchester City because
a Middlesbrough fan had
stolen his shirt.

Q

Macedonian footballer
Mario Gjurovski was sent off
for celebrating a goal by
taking his shorts off
and putting them
on his head.

Fulham striker
Facundo Sava celebrated each
goal by putting on a Zorro mask
that he kept in his sock.

Princess Diana
smuggled sweets into
William and Harry's school
in their football socks.

Haribos contain
nine of the 10 amino acids
essential to humans.

Candy cigarettes
are illegal in France, Spain,
Scandinavia, Portugal, Ireland,
Brazil, Turkey and
Saudi Arabia.

Chocolate milk is
better for you than
a sports drink.

Cockroach milk
is one of the most
nutritious substances
on the planet.

Relative to their size,
cockroaches can run at
210 mph.

Only 52% of the UK's
2,838 speed cameras
are switched on.

A woman
in Oxfordshire has
51 points on her driving licence.

Ant McPartlin
was given the biggest
drink-driving fine in
British history.

To get round the law
that licensed premises must be
a minimum of 500 metres from a highway,
a pub in Kerala constructed a
maze to its front door.

San Marino is
the only country in the world
with more motor vehicles
than people.

A law in Rome
allows any cat to live
undisturbed in its birthplace.

Beatrix Potter
shot a squirrel out of a tree
to provide a model for
Squirrel Nutkin.

It would take
41,923 hazelnuts
to encircle the Coliseum.

In 4th-century Rome,
underpants were
banned.

Florence
hoses down church steps
so tourists don't picnic
on them.

Amsterdam
has a day mayor
and a night mayor.

At a riot in 1766,
the mayor of Nottingham
was knocked over by
a large cheese.

Russia has
a police riot squad
made entirely of sets of
identical twins.

2% of the world's twins
are currently involved in
a scientific study
about twins.

Until the 17th century,
mothers hung their babies
on hooks as they worked.

Prehistoric women
had stronger arms than
members of modern-day
rowing clubs.

Before he became the first person
to row solo across the Atlantic,
John Fairfax was
apprenticed
to a pirate.

Captain Hook
was an Old Etonian
and his last words were
the school motto:
'Floreat Etona.'

Wood-mouse sperm
hook onto one another
to catch a ride.

The longest spider sperm
is twice as long as the
smallest spider.

A *pooter* is a device used
by entomologists to suck insects
into a jar without accidentally
inhaling them.

To *poon* is to prop up
a piece of wobbly furniture
with a wedge under the leg.

Phobophobia is
the fear of developing
a phobia.

Ploitering is
pretending to work
when you aren't.

Scientists are
working on a way
to convert astronauts'
excrement into food.

Henry Ford made it
compulsory for his workers
to go square dancing.

In 2017,
a trade union in
Michigan complained
that goats were taking
its members' jobs.

All UK
postal workers
have to sign the
Official Secrets Act.

Refuse workers
in Turkey have made
a 4,750-volume library
out of discarded books.

Napoleon had a
small portable library
that he called
his 'kindle'.

Braille is
based on a system
devised for Napoleon's army to
help soldiers communicate
in darkness.

You can hear
rhubarb growing
in the dark.

China
is planning
to grow potatoes
on the dark side
of the Moon.

Eating too many
tomatoes can give you
a heart attack.

The world's longest pizza
weighed as much as
an elephant.

Rhinos have
surprisingly dainty feet
and walk on their
insteps.

The Russian for 'step'
is spelled 'шаг' and
pronounced 'shag'.

According to a poll
carried out in Russia,
10% of Russians think
polls are useless.

Russia has
four monuments
to dumplings.

Brussels has a statue
commemorating the place where
Peter the Great
vomited.

Peter the Great
was 6' 8".

NBA star
Manute Bol was
7' 7", but his passport
said he was 5' 2" because he
had been measured sitting down.

The world's
second-tallest person is
a sitting-volleyball player from
Iran who won gold at the
2016 Paralympics.

Medals at the
2016 Paralympics
had small steel balls inside them
so they could be rattled and heard
by visually impaired medallists.

The world land speed record
for a blind motorcyclist
is 165.7 mph.

Australia hosts a World Cup
for Australian Rules football, but
the Australian men's team
doesn't compete because
it wouldn't be fair.

Britain exports
over 50,000 boomerangs to
Australia every year.

The kangaroo rat can
last longer without water
than a camel can.

The Sahara desert
is 10% bigger than it was
100 years ago.

40 million years ago,
a meteorite hit Canada,
raising the temperature to
a record-breaking 2,370°C.

In Venezuela in 1972,
a meteorite killed a cow, but
nobody knew about it because
the farmer ate the cow and used
the meteorite as a doorstop.

Cows with mastitis
are given bras for
their udders.

Pythons
have leg bones.

A rooster
cannot hear
how loud its own
crowing is.

Coral reefs
make a sound like
popcorn being made.

Coral
can drown.

The Breton word
for water is
'dour'.

The Frisian word
for water is
'wetter'.

The air pockets in
an iceberg lettuce are
known as 'goblin caves'.

When an alpaca
gives birth, it is called
an 'unpacking'.

Rats dressed
in polyester trousers
have sex less often than
those made to wear
woollen ones.

By examining the DNA
of any rat in New York,
researchers can tell which
part of the city it comes from.

Manhattan has a monument
commemorating the sinking of the
Staten Island Ferry by a giant octopus,
an event that was entirely
made up by the artist.

15,152 life forms
can be found in the
New York subway.

New York state
has a town called
Lonelyville.

Disenchantment Bay
is a place in
Alaska.

The Useless Islands
belong to New Zealand.

Misery
is a village in France.

Half a billion men in
the world have
depression.

Gloom
swept Finland
on being rated the
world's happiest country.

Rasputin was
happily married
and had seven children.

Rasputin's daughter Maria
grew up to become
a professional
lion tamer.

Frankie Dettori's
mother worked
in a circus.

Warren Buffett
plays the ukulele.

David Beckham
has the Solar System
tattooed on
his head.

Marilyn Manson
collects prosthetics.

The world's
oldest known colour
is pink.

Cough
is Cornish for
'scarlet'.

Isaac Newton's bed,
bed curtains, bedspreads, settee,
easy chair and cushions
were all crimson.

Farmed salmon is white;
the pink is added
artificially.

There are only two
words for colours in the
Bassa language of Liberia:
ziza for warm ones and
hui for cool ones.

6,900 different languages
are spoken in the
world today.

770,000 people
living in England
cannot speak English.

Over 650 languages in India
are not recognised by the state
because they are spoken by
fewer than 10,000 people.

There are
10,000 black holes
at the centre of
our galaxy.

There are 10,000
planes in the sky at
any one time.

One litre of
Dior's J'Adore perfume
contains 10,000 flowers.

10,000 bridges in Italy
are in danger of
collapsing.

It takes
1.3 million cars
to produce as much
carbon dioxide as the UK's
microwave ovens.

You can't melt
a Cadbury's Flake
in a microwave.

Melted chocolate
that has dried on a road
is a worse hazard
than snow.

20% of all the
animal road deaths in
England take place
on the A303.

Gloucester
sends a lamprey pie to
the Queen for each of her jubilees,
but as a protected species in the UK,
the lampreys have to come
from Canada.

Canada
has a strategic
maple-syrup reserve.

Fort Blunder,
built by the US in 1816
to defend itself from Canada,
was accidentally built in Canada.

Bear Castle
is the literal translation
from Swedish of
Björn Borg.

Mahatma Gandhi
wrote in to ask about the
Charles Atlas bodybuilding course.

Krishna Pandit Bhanji is
Sir Ben Kingsley's real name.

Mswati III,
the king of Swaziland,
has changed his country's name
to eSwatini to avoid it
being mistaken for
Switzerland.

In 2007,
the Swiss Army invaded
Liechtenstein by accident:
it was dark, and they couldn't see
where they were going.

In the 15th century,
the Swiss Army used
flutes for signalling.

The longest musical note
in common usage is called
a breve and comes from
the Latin for 'brief'.

Brahms
took 22 years to
write his First Symphony.

A 128th note is called a
semihemidemisemiquaver.

'Full penetration butt weld'
is a technical term used
by metal-workers.

Human beings
are 3% metal.

If two pieces
of metal touch in space,
they stick together.

Valentina Tereshkova,
the first woman in space,
told her family she was going
to a skydiving training camp.
Her mother only found out
the truth from the news.

The dirty clothes
worn by astronauts on
the International Space Station
are jettisoned to burn up on re-entry.

When astronaut
Harrison Schmitt ran for the US Senate,
his opponent's slogan was
'What on Earth has he
done for you lately?'

America's
Prohibition Party has
been on every presidential
ballot paper since 1872.

The Rhinoceros Party of Canada
promised to repeal the law of gravity
and improve higher education by
building taller schools.

Turkish schools
no longer teach
evolution.

Pupils in Ireland
study Irish for 10 years;
outside school, only 1.8% of
the population speak
Irish every day.

Schools in
Wakayama, Japan,
serve whale meatballs
for lunch.

Some schools
in Pennsylvania
have been equipped
with buckets of stones
to throw at armed attackers.

Janis Joplin
was voted the
'ugliest boy in the school'.

Noel Gallagher once broke
Liam Gallagher's foot
with a cricket bat.

The singer-songwriter
Tom Robinson kept poison
in his fridge for 10 years
in case he needed to
kill himself in
the night.

Pop stars aged
between 26 and 35 are
ten times as likely to die
as the rest of us.

Rolling Stone magazine
named the Instagram feed of the US
Transportation Security Administration
the fourth best in the world.

Items confiscated by the
Transportation Security Administration
include a knife inside an enchilada
and a dagger concealed in a
replica Eiffel Tower.

The Leaning Tower of Pisa
took 206 years
to complete.

The bootlace worm is as long as Nelson's Column is tall.

The Ravenmaster
at the Tower of London
whistles a special tune to summon
the ravens to bed each night.

In 1959,
a new language was
discovered in the Pyrenees
that consisted entirely of
ear-splitting whistles.

The Lucerne University
of Applied Sciences and Arts
offers a degree in
yodelling.

He'e holua
is the traditional
Hawaiian sport of
lava sledding.

Skyaking
is the extreme sport
of skydiving in a kayak.

The oldest skydiver is a
101-year-old British
D-Day veteran.

You can scuba dive
underneath
Budapest.

Only 16%
of Hungarians
think they live in a
tolerant nation.

Britons
feel they need
to keep only six of
the Ten Commandments.

Ten-pin bowling
evolved from a German
religious ceremony.

Only two members
of the US Congress say
they don't believe in God.

The bar-tailed godwit
can fly 6,800 miles
without a rest.

Songbirds
get angry when
their rivals are better
at singing.

A blackbird can sing
two songs simultaneously
and harmonise
with itself.

40,000
Highland midges can
land on a single human arm
in one hour.

Asian elephants
have the same female
sex pheromone as
140 species
of moth.

A horse's teeth
take up more space
in its head than
its brain.

Red pandas are the only
non-primate mammals that
can taste artificial
sweeteners.

Pan Pan the panda,
rescued as a cub in 1986,
has since fathered 120 of
the 520 pandas alive
in captivity.

All pandas
born outside China are
repatriated there by Fedex
at about four years old.

[450]

Just four of
Japan's 6,852 islands
make up 97% of its
land area.

The Queen
has travelled
over a million miles.

Prince Charles
is exempt from the
Data Protection Act.

Donald Trump
steams his trousers
while still wearing them.

Chino is
Latin American Spanish
for 'toasted'.

Levi's jeans are
made to look pre-worn
by scorching them
with lasers.

The inventor of the laser
didn't know what
it would be
used for.

The idea of
the midlife crisis was
invented by a Canadian
in London in 1957.

Steel was invented
in India around
400 BC.

The Humber Bridge is
held up by 44,117 miles of steel wire,
enough to circle the world twice.

Christmas Island
has a bridge built
just for crabs.

The carrier crab uses
its back legs to grip a sea urchin,
which it carries on its back
like a shield.

The cloakroom at the
Houses of Parliament has
storage space for MPs' swords,
and at least one MP uses it.

Theresa May was
introduced to her husband
by Benazir Bhutto.

The briefing folder
David Cameron took to
Prime Minister's Questions
was known as the 'plastic fantastic'.

In the last 20 years,
Switzerland has had over
180 referendums.

The Swiss Air Force
is only available during
business hours: 8 a.m. to 6 p.m.

10 trillion business cards
are printed in the US each year,
88% of which are thrown away
within a week of being handed out.

The names of UK businesses
including the word 'Scottish'
outnumber those including
the word 'English'
by four to one.

In 1961,
the co-founder of
Domino's Pizza traded
his 50% stake in the business
for a Volkswagen Beetle.

Only
female bees
can sting.

Jellyfish stinging cells
explode with an acceleration
a million times greater
than a Ferrari's.

Sloths move
three times faster
in water than on land.

When the Arctic sea ice melts,
it will be possible to swim
in a straight line from
Antarctica to
Norway.

Norway's
deepest fjord is
100 metres deeper than
the combined height of the
Empire State Building
and the Burj Khalifa
in Dubai.

The Burj Khalifa,
the world's tallest building,
was built by Samsung.

40 leopards live in Dubai,
and 40% of their diet
is provided by the
city's dogs.

The Mesolithic diet
was mostly
hazelnuts.

Chestnut
was Clyde Barrow of
Bonnie and Clyde's
middle name.

No one knows
why the Finns call
their country
Suomi.

The original
Finnish alphabet
didn't include
the letter 'F'.

Per head of population,
Finland has won more medals
at the Summer Olympics than
any other country.

So they can be shared
with family and friends,
the gold medals designed for
the 2024 Paris Olympics
are divisible into four.

Gold worth $2 million
passes through
Swiss sewers
every year.

Augustus Caesar
sent 10,000 troops
to find the source of the
world's frankincense.

Slugs
hate myrrh.

Lewis Carroll
collected snails.

In 2008,
a new species of insect
was discovered in the garden of
the Natural History Museum
by a five-year-old boy.

Indian jumping ants
can smell which of the
larvae will mature
into a queen.

Queen Victoria
hung a photograph
of Prince Albert on his deathbed
over every bed she slept in.

In 1926,
the future George VI
competed in the men's doubles
at Wimbledon, but was knocked out
in his first match.

Cricketers
wore a box to protect their
genitals for more than 100 years
before they wore a helmet
to protect their head.

In Finland,
they make bread
from crickets.

Elephants have
three times as many
brain cells as
humans.

Edward VII
had a golf bag made
from an elephant's penis.

Donald Trump's
golf bag contains
high-powered rifles,
as well as clubs.

The average plastic bag
gets used for 12 minutes but
takes up to 1,000 years
to biodegrade.

Eating a bag
of crisps a day for
a year is equivalent to
drinking five litres
of cooking oil.

Snakes
that eat snakes
can eat snakes that
are 139% of their
own length.

The smallest known snake
is the size of a
toothpick.

In 2017,
snakes were observed
hunting in packs for
the first time.

Snakes are
not allowed on
American Airlines planes
as emotional support
animals.

The Americans
most likely to use fonts
that look like handwriting
are Nevadans.

Comic Sans is
based on lettering from
the *Watchmen* comics.

In graphic design,
the use of too many
mismatched fonts is called
'the ransom note effect'.

The 'third-person effect'
is the belief that advertising
only convinces
other people.

The 'bystander effect'
is where a person does
nothing in a crisis because
they think someone else will.

New members of the
British royal family undergo
hostage simulation training.

The Royal Navy
is half the size it was
in 1990.

During the Cold War,
to plan for a nuclear meltdown
Russia, Sweden and Finland dusted off
their old steam locomotives.

Siderodromophobia
is the fear of trains.

Aibohphobia
is the fear of palindromes.

People can
overcome phobias if
they're given cash every time
they think about the thing
they're scared of.

£200,000 in loose change
is found on public transport
in London each year.

2,400
phone boxes in Britain
are listed as 'historic landmarks'.

L. Frank Baum,
author of *The Wizard of Oz*,
predicted the smartphone
in 1926.

Steve Jobs
launched the iPhone in 2007
by making a prank call
to Starbucks.

The area code for
Cape Canaveral
is 3–2–1.

Snoopy
is NASA's
official safety mascot.

NASA has
green-lit a project to
create swarms of robot bees
to explore Mars.

A bee's brain
weighs less than
a milligram.

The inventor of M&M's
was allergic to peanuts.

Candyfloss
was invented
by a dentist.

The price tag
was invented by
the Quakers.

In the 1950s,
Quaker Oats gave away
one square inch of land in Canada
with every box sold.

The Vikings
ate frozen food.

The Netherlands
is Europe's biggest
importer of
insects.

1 in 200 Slovenians
keep bees.

Aphids are
born pregnant.

Toenail fungus
is asexual.

Astronauts often
lose their fingernails
after space walks.

Children who bite their nails
are less likely to develop
allergies as an adult.

Mango skins contain
the same allergen
as poison ivy.

Napoleon
was allergic
to leather.

When George Washington died,
Napoleon ordered 10 days
of mourning in France.

Winston Churchill's funeral
was planned under the code name
Operation Hope Not.

The middle name of
17th-century English economist
Nicholas Barbon was If-Christ-had-not-
died-for-thee-thou-hadst-been-damned.

The full name of Thing
from *The Addams Family*
is Thing T. Thing.

Louisa Adams, the wife of the
sixth US president, John Quincy Adams,
is the only First Lady apart from
Melania Trump not to have
been born in the US.

Newborn babies
have half as much chance of
developing asthma if there's
a cat in the house.

When huskies sleep,
they curl up with their tail
over their nose, which traps
the heat against their bodies.

One-third of the energy
a python gets from a meal
goes on digesting
the meal.

The world's largest wine cellar has
underground streets 150 miles long,
where staff and tourists get about
by bike, car and bus.

The world's
largest wine cellar
and the world's second-
largest wine cellar are
both in Moldova.

As much Prosecco is
drunk in the UK each year
as the annual rainfall on
Wembley stadium.

Britain's first
professional footballer
had only one eye.

An Australian law student has
fought a five-year battle to have
a drawing of a cock and balls
officially recognised as his
legal signature.

T. S. Eliot
coined the word
'bullshit'.

In 2017,
the World Taekwondo Federation
changed its name to World Taekwondo
because of the 'negative connotations'
associated with its initials.

Sumo
is Japanese for
'rushing at each other'.

Professional sumo wrestlers
aren't allowed to drive.

If a woman enters
a sumo ring, it has to be
cleaned immediately
with salt.

After iodine was
added to salt in 1924,
the average American IQ
jumped by 15%.

Butterflies can
get the salt they need
by drinking the tears
from turtles' eyes.

TV naturalist
Steve Irwin (1962–2006)
and Charles Darwin (1809–82)
owned the same tortoise.

Lizards were
defined by Dr Johnson as
'an animal resembling a serpent,
with legs added to it'.

Each leg of an
offshore wind turbine
may have up to 4.3 tonnes
of mussels clinging to it.

St David's
is Britain's smallest
and windiest city.

For its size,
Britain has more
tornadoes than any other
country in the world.

The average warning time
for a tornado is
13 minutes.

The average Briton
spends a year of their
working life
off sick.

A quarter
of British nurses
are obese.

To *nurdle* is to muse
on a subject you know
nothing about.

To *snerdle* is to
wrap up cosily
in bed.

A *petarade* is
a series of farts.

Ninguid is
a 17th-century word
for 'snowy'.

Part of
Antarctica is
called the Kodak Gap
because it is so beautiful
it's impossible to take
a bad photo there.

The US Postal Service
photographs every one
of the 160 billion items
of US mail a year.

Jeff Bezos has
been photographed
eating an iguana.

Oscar Wilde
tore off and ate
a corner of each page
after he'd read it.

The *NME* was
originally called
the *Accordion Times*.

Freddy Mercury's original title
for 'Bohemian Rhapsody' was
'The Cowboy Song'.

The song 'Mahna Mahna',
made famous by the Muppets,
was written for a porn film.

Paul McCartney
once spent three hours in prison
for setting a condom
on fire.

Steve Jobs tried to
change the name of the
Apple Macintosh to
the Apple Bicycle.

The tank
was nearly called
'the cistern' or 'the reservoir'.

In the 17th century,
magpies were called
'pie-maggots'.

A sequin
was originally
a gold coin from Italy.

In 1929,
Italy's Fascist government
banned the use of
foreign words.

Cumhracht
is Irish for the
smell of a man's body
after intercourse.

Emmanuel Macron,
president of France,
spends the equivalent
of £24,000 a year
on make-up.

In camel beauty contests,
competitors are disqualified
if they use Botox.

In the 1880s,
thousands of spectators flocked to
newspaper typesetting competitions.

To design a new
English-language font
requires about 230 separate
elements called 'glyphs';
to make a Chinese one
needs over 13,000.

The Glyptodon
was an ancient armadillo
the size of a Volkswagen Beetle
whose shell was large enough
for humans to live in.

As a teenager,
Xi Jinping, president of China,
lived in a cave.

Neanderthals
used glue.

Wallets
were first used
to carry meat.

All the iron
in Bronze Age
tools and weapons came
from meteorites.

At least
200 meteorites
on Earth are known
to have come
from Mars.

Every day,
800 million viruses
fall on each square metre
of the Earth's surface.

The MRSA virus
can be treated with
an Anglo-Saxon potion
that is 1,000 years old.

The antibiotic vancomycin
comes from soil on
the jungle floor
in Borneo.

The rainforest floor
gets less than 3% of the light
that the treetops do.

American tree populations
are steadily moving west, and
no one knows why.

No one knows why
shower curtains
cling to you.

In his late 60s,
Ulysses S. Grant claimed
that no one had seen him
naked since he was
a young child.

When *Spy* magazine
sent cheques for 13 cents to
some of the world's richest people,
no one cashed them except a
Saudi arms dealer and
Donald Trump.

Bankruptcy is
likely to be as fatal
as heart disease.

A fatal dose
of water is
six litres.

A fatal dose of caffeine
is 113 cups of coffee, but
you'd die of water
poisoning first.

Nestlé sells
56 different brands
of water.

Watering plants
with club soda makes them
grow faster and go a nicer
shade of green.

As long as you use soap,
washing your hands works
just as well if the
water is cold.

Mano a mano
means 'hand to hand',
not 'man to man'.

The Island of Misunderstanding
got its name because it was missed
by a map-making expedition.

The first
Americans
came from Siberia.

The earliest known song
was written in
Syria.

Cougars
have a cry
that sounds like a
woman screaming.

Australian magpies
can understand what
other birds are
saying.

Pelicans
swallow pigeons
whole.

Hedgehogs
hunt and kill
adders.

Coconut crabs
climb trees and
hunt birds.

Quetzal birds
eat avocados whole
but regurgitate the stone
because it makes them
too heavy to take off.

You can lose weight by
leaving your bedroom window
open at night.

There are more
possible arrangements
of a deck of cards than
there are stars in the
known universe.

Children
asked to draw stars
instinctively draw
five of them.

The human eye can detect
a single photon.

A single violin
is made from over 70
pieces of wood.

Christchurch, New Zealand,
has a 700-seat cathedral
made of cardboard.

Cardboard was
invented in China
before the birth of Christ.

The nail
was invented
by the ancient Romans.

Scientists
can't decide on
the definition of a tree.

Hawaiian violets
have wooden stems.

Physicists at the
University of Hawaii
have solved the problem of
how washing machines
get clothes clean.

Washing Machine – The Movie
is a 66-minute-long single shot of
a wash, rinse and spin cycle, with
a score by Michael Nyman.

There are more
vending machines in Japan
than there are people
in New Zealand.

The Japanese
for 'achoo!' is
hakashun!

The Filipino
for 'achoo!' is
haching!

Deaf people
don't say 'achoo!'
when they sneeze.

The droplets
in a single cough
can contain 200 million
virus particles.

Cough mixture in Qatar
must be prescribed
by a doctor.

Vicks VapoRub
is illegal in Japan,
Greece and Singapore.

No one knows
how aspirin works.

British pensions are so
complicated that not even the
chief economist of the Bank of England
understands them.

Membership of the
Royal Bastards Society
is open to anyone who can
prove illegitimate descent
from a king of England,
Wales or Scotland.

James IV of Scotland
paid people to let him
extract their teeth.

The Queen
travels everywhere with
a black mourning suit,
just in case.

The French Foreign Legion
has its own vineyard.

90% of wines are
meant to be drunk
within a year.

Britons in 2018
buy six times as many
cups of coffee as they
did in 2000.

Postgraduate students
are six times as depressed
as the rest of us.

Every year spent
in secondary education
adds 11 months to the
length of your life.

The Ethiopian calendar
has 13 months.

Franklin D. Roosevelt
refused to travel on
Friday the 13th.

45% of the
world's cargo ships are
travelling empty.

Fishing boats
cast their nets over
55% of the ocean's surface.

Only 34% of the
world's land surface is
used for any kind
of agriculture.

The Gobi Desert
is twice the size
of France.

The world's
smallest desert
covers one square mile.

The circumference
of the world was estimated
by Eratosthenes of Cyrene
2,000 years ago, and he
was only 1% out.

All the Slinkys
ever made would
encircle the world
150 times.

The inventor of the Slinky
ran away to join a
religious cult.

In 2015,
the Vatican performed
an exorcism on the whole
of Mexico.

The Australian constitution
includes New Zealand
as its seventh state.

The Hungarian constitution
was drafted on
an iPad.

The US constitution is
the only one from
the 18th century
still in use.

The Irish
for USA is
SAM.

Hitler's nephew,
William Hitler, served
in the US Navy.

Before the Second World War,
the US Navy trained on the assumption
that it would have to fight
the Royal Navy next.

Japan's
Self-Defence Forces
have a larger navy than
Britain and France combined
but have never fired
a shot in battle.

Samurai
always brought
dried plums to
battles.

Asparagus tips
are called
'squibs'.

Concrete
is stronger if
carrots are added to it.

When the first avocados
were sold by Marks & Spencer,
they came with a leaflet
explaining how
to eat them.

All strawberries today
derive from five plants brought
to France from Chile in 1712.

France has
a larger economy
than the whole of Africa.

99.99% of the territory
of the Cook Islands
is open sea.

Tahitian has
no word for
'sadness'.

The parliament
of Palau is called
the House of Whispers.

The oceans
are getting louder.

Ferns
are older
than seeds.

Darkness
moves faster
than light.

There's no such thing
as total darkness
anywhere in the
universe.

24 Thanks

A huge thank you to our friends and colleagues at QI – Alex Bell, Rob Blake, Alexey Boronenko, Will Bowen, Edward Brooke-Hitching, Jack Chambers, Mat Coward, Alice Campbell Davis, Jenny Doughty, Chris Emerson, Mandy Fenton, Piers Fletcher, Lauren Gilbert, Emily Jupitus, Coco Lloyd, John Mitchinson, Andrew Hunter Murray, Justin Pollard, Anna Ptaszynski, James Rawson, Dan Schreiber, Liz Townsend and Mike Turner.

And a very special thank you to our marvellous editor Laura Hassan and to Faber & Faber, who have been home to QI's books from the beginning.

Index

This is here to help you find your favourite bits.
Like the facts themselves, we've kept it as simple as we can.

431; Alaska–Yukon–Pacific Exposition 157; Albania 181; Prince Albert 460; albums 195; Albuquerque 96; alcohol 17, 62, 98, 127, 233; ale houses 75; Alexa 125; Alfred the Butler 12; algorithms 258; 'All I Want for Christmas Is You' 89; all-day breakfast 329; Jason Allen 265; allergens 471; allergies 219, 359, 468, 471; alliances 147; alligators 201; alpacas 429; alphabets 146, 458; altered states 2; Alutiiq people 156; Alzheimer's 215, 278; amateurs 28; Amazon 125, 251; ambition 199; American Airlines 333, 463; American Civil War 91, 92; American Coffee Bureau 11; American football 207, 372; American Kitchen Foods 52; American Revolutionary War 131; Americans 61, 63, 85, 117, 182, 193, 202, 209, 254, 261, 299, 310, 313, 350, 368, 393, 405, 464, 476, 490; amino acids 413; amnesiacs 215; amphibians 125; amphibious 216, 347; amputations 24; Amsterdam 417; anacondas 265; anaesthetics 311; ancient China 209, 346, 493; ancient Egypt 18, 19, 57, 63, 354; ancient Greece 25, 42, 107, 186, 211, 237, 374; ancient Greek 145, 166, 301; ancient Peru 38; ancient Rome 116, 180, 221, 262, 276, 307, 417, 493; André the Giant 46; Julie Andrews 328; anger 449; angina 61; Anglo-Saxons 360, 486; animal kingdom 411; animals 132, 138, 175, 194, 268, 395, 402, 437; *Anne of Geierstein* 336; Anne of Green Gables 300; annoying 140, 286; anonymity 107; Antarctic sea spiders 268; Antarctica 31, 153, 203, 268, 456, 480; anthrax 350; anti-bacterial 43; antibiotics 139, 318, 486; anticlockwise 255; antifreeze 378; antimatter 96; antisocial 230; ants 181, 189, 343; ants' nests 217; anus-loss 279; Aosta Valley 377; aphids 470; Apollo 11 15; apologies 54, 250; applause 178; Apple 3, 60, 219; Apple III 351; Apple Bicycle 482; Apple Mac 67, 482; apples 3, 219, 328; applications 108; appointments 252; apprentices 419; Arab countries 10;

Archaeopteryx 56; Arctic 158, 456; area 88, 273, 300, 451, 500; area codes 467; Argentina 97, 345; argon 211; aristocracy coordinators 400; Aristotle 64; armadillos 306, 484; armed attackers 443; Armenia 26, 301; armpits 57; arms 231, 253, 354, 418, 449; arms dealers 487; Neil Armstrong 108; army officers 384; arrangements 323, 492; arrests 75, 85, 168, 190, 192, 197, 205, 285, 321, 370; Arsenal 201; arses 163; arson 85; artificial colours 434; artificial mounds 30; artificial sweeteners 450; artificial trees 77; artists 166, 430; artworks 312; Asbest, Russia 33; asbestos mines 33; asexuality 470; ash 287; ashes 154; ashtrays 355; Asia 66; Asian elephants 449; asparagus tips 504; aspens 103; aspirin 496; assembling 354; asthma 350, 473; Aston Martin 79; astronauts 108, 109, 155, 182, 254, 421, 442, 471; astronomers 336; atheism 252; athletes 107; Atlantic 31, 419; Atlas 269; Charles Atlas 439; ATMs 317; David Attenborough 28; Richard Attenborough 400; attractions 235; attractiveness 105; aubergines 130; auctions 180, 263, 312; Augustus Caesar 459; Australia 30, 66, 113, 269, 362, 363, 404, 426, 475, 502; Australian 147; Australian black kites 279; Australian magpies 490; Australian Rules football 426; Austria 184; Austrian Army 213; authors 143, 317; autobiographies 317; auto-brewery syndrome 379; autocorrections 52; autumn 372; avalanches 357; Avian Science and Conservation Centre 380; avocados 26, 173, 361, 491, 504; awake 338; Azerbaijan 301; Aztecs 194, 306

babies 58, 104, 125, 326, 396, 397, 418, 473; Babu 120; Babylonians 23; backs 373, 453; backwards words 295; bacon and eggs 12; bacteria 41, 139, 369, 371; badgers 162; badges 347; baguette deliveries 376; *Bake Off* 301; Baker Island 344; Bakerloo Line 343; baking 297; Baku 78; balancing 314;

baldness 44; Lucille Ball 109; Balmoral 85; Baltimore 96; Baluchistan 212; bamboo sharks 14; bananas 180, 181, 265; Bangkok 360; Bangladesh 88, 172; bank 183; Bank of England 497; bankruptcy 488; banks 225, 387; bans 9, 100, 111, 150, 160, 193, 231, 233, 240, 325, 336, 384, 404, 417, 483; Bantu 106; 'bar code men' 44; barbers 115, 175; Nicholas Barbon 472; bar codes 252; bards 253; Bark Rangers 235; barking 102, 103; Barry 101; bar-tailed godwits 448; Joey Barton 412; Gavin Barwell 178; baseball 290, 291; bashful bladder syndrome 368; basketball 273, 352; basketball players 411; baskets 131, 266; Bassa language 435; Bassian thrushes 66; bastardium 280; Letitia Bat 286; bathhouses 240; bathing 240, 408; Batman 13; bats 123, 241, 291, 308, 331, 402; battle 391, 503; battle cries 247; battlefields 131; Mr Baubles 77; L. Frank Baum 467; Bayeux Tapestry 80; BBC 274; beached whales 385; beagles 122, 162; beaks 70, 156; beans 63, 64; Bear Castle 438; beards 61, 110; bears 124, 188; beastly 164; The Beatles 21, 112, 132, 191, 281; beauty 480; beauty contests 483; Dorothy Beck 14; Samuel Beckett 46; David Beckham 433; bed curtains 434; Bedfordshire Clanger 298; bedrooms 492; beds 434, 460, 479; beef 349, 408; beef soup 408; Beefeaters 408; Beefsteak Chapel 26; bee-keeping 470; beer 47, 240, 315, 316, 388; beer kegs 48; beer mats 47, 165, 397; bees 154, 306, 356, 456, 468; beetles 112; Mrs Beeton 111; Belgium 257, 321; Bell End 86; Bellagio 191; Bellagio hotel 191; bell-ringing peals 206; bells 206, 224, 363; Pope Benedict XVI 384; Bentley 223; Berlin 232, 309; Irving Berlin 229; Bermuda 320, 340; Bermuda shorts 340; Bert 410; Anna Bertha 231; best friends 297; bestsellers 111, 281, 317; betting 388; Beyoncé 195, 399; Jeff Bezos 480; Bhutan 18, 166; Benazir Bhutto 454; Bible 65, 383, 386; bicycle tyres

bottoms 20, 39, 194; bounties 395; Ansel Bourne 215; Jason Bourne 215; Bournemouth 253; Sean Bowen 359; bowhead whales 385; David Bowie 109; bowls 352, 398; boxes 461; boys 134; Johannes Brahms 440; braille 422; brain cells 461; brain damage 283; brain surgery 23; brains 121, 211, 283, 307, 450, 468; brainwaves 114; brakes 347; Bramley apples 219; brand names 332; branding 49; brands 488; Brandt's bat 402; bras 360, 427; Brazil 65, 194, 235, 414; bread 336, 461; breadth 282; breakfast 143; breasts 159; breathalysers 17; breath-holding 396; breathing 58, 59, 114, 185, 384; breeching parties 17; breeding 224; Breton 429; breves 440; breweries 315, 316; bribes 167; bridges 92, 436, 453; briefing folders 454; Britain 40, 146, 147, 172, 185, 269, 275, 292, 293, 310, 315, 329, 412, 416, 467, 478, 503; British Airways 355; British Army 43, 88, 98; British Association of Dermatologists 272; British Christmas Tree Growers' Association 77; British Lawnmower Museum 359; British Ornithologists' Union 399; Britons 8, 54, 63, 67, 143, 379, 408, 448, 478, 498; Brno 241; broadcasts 199; Broadway 254; broccoli 170; Bronze Age 485; Brooklyn 325; brothers 42, 155; brown widow spiders 342; brown wrappers 407; Bruce 32; Brummie of the Year 120; brunettes 264; Brussels 424; buckets 216, 443; Duke of Buckingham 115; Francis Buckland 260; Budapest 447; Henry Budd 202; Buddhism 231; budgie smugglers 240; budgies 267, 357; Budweiser 397; Warren Buffett 433; building 184; buildings 89, 116, 148, 352, 457; bulging 227; bulletproof 230; bullfighters 248; bullshit 475; bullying 134; bumblebees 87; bunches 265; burger buns 406; burial 90, 97, 242, 253, 390; Burj Khalifa 457; burning 287; Bus Driver 8; buses 474; business cards 455; business hours 455; businesses 455; bussing in 76; butchers 357; Jimmy Butler 273; butter

335; Cumberland Clark 253; classification 174; classmates 35; clay 223; clean 494; cleaning 344, 476; cleaning products 15, 221; Nick Clegg 274; clergy 110; click beetles 248; climate change 82, 203, 224; climbing 272, 283, 491; clinging 487; Bill Clinton 137; cloakrooms 454; clocks 255; clockwork rovers 109; 'Close Door' buttons 15; closures 22; cloth 358; clothes 80, 82, 126, 170, 222, 230, 287, 341, 442, 494; club soda 489; Clytoris 360; coaches 198, 352; coal 287; coastlines 79, 113; coats 193; coca leaves 83; Coca-Cola 181, 200, 309, 389; cocaine 83, 304, 305; cock and balls 475; cockroach milk 414; cockroaches 414; cocktails 127, 305; coconut crabs 369, 491; coconut shell 171; code names 472; codes 238; coding 67, 237; coffee 5, 6, 24, 266, 318, 341, 366, 488, 498; coffee breaks 11; coffee cups 216; coffee houses 209; coffee pods 209; coffee stirrers 402; coffin clubs 95; coffins 95; coinages 43, 145, 475; coins 51, 52, 243, 244; cold 118, 138, 378, 379, 489; Cold War 465; colds 349; Colgate 208; Coliseum 416; collapsing 436; collections 245, 246, 307; collective nouns 183, 222, 377; collectors 214, 232, 433, 460; Colombo airport 197; colour TV 28; colours 258, 322, 341, 348, 434, 435; Christopher Columbus 13; combing 61, 147; combovers 44; Comic Sans 464; comics 464; commoners 352; communication 289, 422; company ownership 100; compasses 346; competitions 298, 484; complicated 497; composing 67; compulsory 240; computer games 327, 391; computer simulations 294; computers 67, 205, 351; computing power 48; Sir Arthur Conan Doyle 11; concentration 244; conception 104, 281; concepts 288; concerts 247; Concorde 41, 182; concrete 401, 504; condensed milk 216; conditions 202; condoms 174, 481; conferences 252; confiscated items 445; confusion 411; congregations 338; Connecticut 285,

cysts 162; Czech 241; Czech Republic 44, 240, 241, 339; Czechoslovakia 68

Jack Dagger 357; daggers 363, 445; damage 333; damsels 246; dancing 64, 106, 228, 277, 284; 'Dancing Queen' 277; dandelion trees 405; dandruff 139; danger 5, 68, 233; darcin 105; Mr Darcy 105, 401; darkness 70, 422, 439, 506; Charles Darwin 477; Data Protection Act 451; dating 105; dating profiles 27, 239; daughters 432; Joe Davis 352; day 171, 417; Day of the Dead 130; days 18; D-Day veterans 447; dead 258, 348; dead people 24, 215, 284, 391; Dead Salmon 258; deadlines 108; deafness 41, 247, 495; dealers 285; death 231, 235, 259, 297, 318, 444; death row 290; death sentence 54, 55, 99; deathbeds 460; death-metal bands 260; deaths 74, 131, 164, 274; death's head hawk moths 260; Claude Debussy 327; debuts 412; decaf coffee 6; declarations of independence 299; decommissioning 167; decomposition 242; decorations 299; decrees 135, 161, 358; Deep Purple 247; deep-frying 118; deer 103, 303; defecating 362; Defence Against the Dark Arts 164; definitions 72, 397, 477, 494; DEFRA 217; degrade 462; degrees 446; Delaware River 291; delays 290, 322, 355; demilitarised zones 394; democracies 202; demons 93; demotions 88; Denmark 97, 146, 167, 303; density 278; dentists 469; Department of Health 81; depression 221, 316, 432, 498; descent 234; descriptions 315; deserts 45, 500; desiccation 15; designers 60, 86, 214, 354; desks 347; destroyers 356; destruction 205; detachable heads 262; detection 312, 492; detergent 256; Detroit 285; Frankie Dettori 433; Deutsche Bank 184; Devil 398; Devil's Breath 93; The Devil's Point 93; Melville Dewey 136; Dewey Decimal System 136; Dexter 333; Timothy Dexter 353;

diagnoses 215; Diagram Prize 84; dialects 163, 198; Diamond Jubilee 12; diamonds 96; Princess Diana 413; diarrhoea 172; diets 127, 457; difficulty 2, 197; digesting 334, 473; diners 112, 353; dining-room tables 357, 386; dinner jackets 340; dinosaurs 56, 139, 225, 232, 263, 264; Diocletian 180; Dior 436; directors 198, 324, 357, 380; dirty thunderstorms 392; disagreements 291; discoveries 25, 82, 213, 446, 460; disease 37; Disenchantment Bay 431; disguises 149; disgusting 407; disinterring 90, 284; Dismal Swamps 404; Disney 294, 295; D'Isney 295; Disneyland 22; disorganisation 2; disposable cups 216, 217; disqualification 483; distillation 211; distractions 193; disturbing 268, 416; diving 372; divining rods 98; divorce rates 16; Novak Djokovic 388; DNA 236, 430; Do Not Disturb 214; dockyard oysters 171; *Dr Jekyll and Mr Hyde* 253; Dr Pepper 200; *Dr Strangelove* 22; *Doctor Who* 301; doctors 11, 61, 62, 152, 496; documentaries 67; Ken Dodd 208; dog breeds 293; dog food 176; dog shows 271; dogging 274; dogs 80, 97, 100, 101, 131, 132, 189, 234, 249, 294, 351, 366, 369, 370, 383, 457; doing nothing 465; doll's houses 407; dolphins 154, 247; domain names 300; domes 319; Domesday Book 12; Domino's Pizza 455; Donald Duck 228; donations 166; donkeys 147, 330; donkey's milk 406; Door Sniffer 160; doors 70, 247; doorstops 427; Doris 25; Fyodor Dostoevsky 10; dough 135; doughnuts 325; downdraughts 328; drafting 502; dragon clouds 148; dragons 148, 239; drawers 106; drawing 252, 289, 475, 492; dreams 281, 382, 383; dressing 13, 170, 222, 430; dried fruit 95; dried plums 503; drilling 385; drink-driving 205, 221, 415; drinking 6, 42, 47, 57, 58, 74, 221, 260, 366, 389, 462, 474, 476, 498; drivers 30, 38, 46; driving 68, 142, 273, 329, 347, 393, 476; driving licences 415; drones 70; droplets 496; drowning 315, 428;

83, 334, 363; energy 68, 69, 473; engineers 98, 254; England 64, 77, 126, 161, 195, 242, 390, 435, 497; England (surname) 128; English 2, 107, 146, 198, 253, 435, 455, 484; enjoyment 64, 139, 345; Brian Eno 67; *Enterprise* 247; entomologists 420; envelopes 116, 247; environment 77, 209; epileptic fits 311; equal-pay protests 50; equators 227; Eratosthenes of Cyrene 501; Ernest 157; Ernie 410; escalators 313; escaping 64, 120, 135, 279; estimation 501; eSwatini 439; Ethiopia 499; Eton 419; EU 322; Europe 322, 470; euros 263; Eurovision Song Contest 185, 301; Euston 115; Everest 30, 186, 283; evolution 5, 443; exclamation marks 353; excrement 279, 280, 381, 421; excuses 365; executions 290; exemptions 451; exfoliation 385; exhaling 234; exorcisms 384, 501; expeditions 489; experiments 367; exploding trousers 178; exploring 335, 468; explosions 87; explosives 179, 220; exporting 426; expressions 145, 147, 188, 244, 317; Extra Crispy Sunscreen 272; extreme sports 447; eye patches 374; eyeballs 176; eyebrows 5, 410; eyelids 175; eyeline 307; eyes 2, 14, 19, 20, 45, 121, 126, 175, 334, 474, 476, 492; eyes in the sky 96

'F' 458; Peter Carl Fabergé 36; faces 343; facial expressions 370, 383; factories 217; fading 337; faecal bacteria 114; John Fairfax 419; fairies 391; fakes 48, 94, 252, 315; falconers 223; falcons 259; falling 226, 313, 324; falling out 155, 276; falls survived 188; families 192, 406; fan blades 314; fan clubs 219, 399; fangs 261; Fanny Hands Lane 159; fans 399; *Fantastic Beasts and Where to Find Them* 164; Fantasy Football 294; fantasy spiders 331; *Fargo* 229; farmed salmon 434; farmers 158, 181, 241, 427; farming 200, 201, 242; farmworkers 119; Farrow & Ball 258; farts 66, 227,

228, 308, 311, 479; Fascism 483; fashionable 290; *Fast and the Furious* 134, 273; fatal 488; fatal doses 488; fathers 327, 398, 450; fatness 236; fault-finding 365; favour 262; fear 144, 154, 198, 310, 370, 420, 466; feathers 57, 70, 264; February 360; Fedex 450; fees 140; feet 135, 261, 283, 351, 423; Félicette 308; Ferdinand of Bulgaria 144; Ferdinand I of Naples 82; fermented nectar 127; ferns 506; Ferrari 456; ferrets 179; Ferris wheels 33; fiction 336; *Fight Club* 324; fighter pilots, 248; fighter planes 248; fights 277, 377; Filipino 495; film adaptations 401; film genres 229; film titles 229; filming 156, 265; films 114, 130, 134, 161, 164, 191, 246, 400; financial news 321; David Fincher 324; fines 115, 129, 242, 415; fingernails 391, 471; fingerprints 32, 37, 97; fingers 97; Finland 99, 153, 212, 432, 458, 461, 465; *Finnegans Wake* 373; Finnish 106, 458; fire fighters 85; Fireman Sam 85; fires 85, 279, 481; firing 198; firing squads 99; first dates 339; First Ladies 473; first names 128, 136, 158; first taste 397; first words 164; First World War 99, 115, 144, 179, 315, 362; fish 14, 52, 53, 117, 126, 257; fish scales 141; fish substitutes 379; fish-and-chip shops 53, 126; Fisher-Price 348; fishing 53, 379; fishing boats 500; fitness 326; five 492; five-star hotels 184, 263; fjords 457; flags 213, 214, 361; flatulence 61; flight instruments 356; flightless birds 344; floating 403; flooding 18; Florence 417; Florida 48; flowering 250; flowers 436; flu viruses 350; fluorescence 309; flushing toilets 134; flutes 49, 440; fly repellent 221; fly swatters 57; Flybe 356; flying 41, 48, 182, 264, 302, 325, 448; flying foxes 102; foetuses 37; folding stools 354; fonts 464, 484; food 14, 20, 61, 176, 192, 345, 397, 421; food poisoning 350; food supply 138, 185; food-grinding 102; fooling 14; football 9, 10, 29, 73, 202, 372; football commentators 222;

galloping 264; gallows 99; gamblers 149; gambling 150; *Game of Thrones* 34; games 150, 388, 389, 390; Mahatma Gandhi 439; gardeners 46; gas-mask filters 362; gauntlet compartments 223; GDP 300; geese 97, 222, 381; gender imbalance 229; generals 131; genetic engineering 261, 346; genetics 293, 326, 343; Geneva 263; genitals 174, 185, 461; Genoa airport 270; George V 239; George VI 21, 212, 461; Georgia 322; German 25, 35, 128, 296, 316; Germany 115, 129, 144, 151, 167, 321, 325, 448; George Gershwin 274; G-force 248; Ghana 314; ghost costumes 149; ghosts 25, 149, 285; giant armadillos 281; giant pandas 41; gifts 160, 228; gin 328; gin and tonic 74; ginger 264; giraffes 57, 264; *The Girl with the Dragon Tattoo* 239; Mario Gjurovski 413; glaciers 226, 272; Glasgow 5, 93; glass 22; glasses 47, 364; Glastonbury festival 89; gloom 432; Gloucester 438; Gloucestershire 72; glow 45, 70, 329; glue 485; gluten-free 336; glyphs 484; Glyptodons 484; gnashing 386; goal celebrations 413; goats 88, 89, 194, 421; Gobi Desert 500; goblin caves 429; God 63, 97, 448; goddesses 231; gods 25, 26, 63; gold 49, 95, 197, 381, 459; gold coins 482; gold nuggets 225; Jeff Goldblum 142; goldfish 257, 375; Goldman Sachs 52; golf bag 462; gondola rides 22; good luck 141; Google 205, 252, 281, 372; Google Maps 117; gooseberry bush 210; goosebumps 368; gossips 210; got the morbs 210; gout 61; Graham crackers 323; grampussing 216; *Grand Theft Auto V* 134; Cary Grant 198; Ulysses S. Grant 92, 370, 487; grants 252; grapes 304; graphic design 464; grass 269, 359; grasshoppers 46; grass-trimming 169; gravestones 284; grave-tending 339; gravity 226; gravy 305; Great Barrier Reef 318; Great Indian Bustards 136; Greece 26, 496; green 58, 193, 275, 489; green man 394; green tea 118;

Greenland 300; greetings 351; grey 374; Greyhound buses 270; Grinch 77; grocery bags 298; groins 234; grooming 209; grottoes 384; growing 7, 121, 161, 267, 304, 369, 422, 423, 489; grubs 139; grunts 387; guacamole 27; Guam 187; guards 97; Guelph 128; guests 80, 386, 408; Che Guevara 97; Guggenheim Museum 381; guide horses 370; guidelines 168; guillemots 58; Guinness 316; Guinness World Records 188, 314; guitars 51; Gulf corvina fish 247; Gunpowder Plot 384; gyms 370

Habeas Corpus Act 220; habitats 96, 224; haemorrhoids 61; hailing 260; hair 61, 109, 280; hair conditioner 168; hair loss 372; haircuts 115; hair-pulling 372; hairspray 271; hairstyles 44; Haiti 213; Hallstatt 184; hammerhead worms 66; hammers 172; hamsters 377; Han (river) 116; Matt Hand 397; hand grenades 171; hand to hand 489; hand-cupping 398; hand-dryers 114; handedness 101; hand-holding 114; handkerchiefs 358; H&M 287; hands 4, 37, 97, 114, 138, 180, 216, 231, 290, 397; handshakes 4, 56; handsome men 345; handspan 398; hand-washing 489; handwriting 464; hanging 99; hangovers 42; Hanoi 6, 395; happiness 363, 394, 432; hard drives 205; Warren Harding 80; Thomas Hardy 11, 407; harems 94; Haribos 413; harmonising 449; Harrods 100, 304; Prince Harry 413; Harry Potter films 164, 331; hat etiquette 21, 34; Hatebeak 260; hatpins 242; hats 38, 91, 140; hauntings 284; Havana airport 48; 'Have You Been?' 232; Hawaii 400, 446; Hawaiian violets 494; Stephen Hawking 373; hawks 259; hay fever 153; hazards 437; hazelnuts 416, 457; headaches 61; headphone jacks 230; heads 42, 126, 127, 215, 314, 343, 401, 405, 433, 450, 461; healing 171, 318; health 74, 118, 414; Seamus Heaney 198; hearing 37, 422, 428; heart attacks

200, 209, 216, 222, 252, 351, 352, 360, 393, 452, 468, 501;
investors 202; invisible ink 321; invisible posters 321; Io
227; iodine 476; iPads 502; iPhones 60, 467; IQ 285, 476;
Iran 168, 340, 425; Iraq 394; Ireland 165, 250, 414, 443; Irish
163, 198, 313, 316, 443, 483, 502; iron 485; irritating 286;
Steve Irwin 477; Isigny 295; Island of Love 113; Island of
Misunderstanding 489; islands 72, 113, 451; Isle of Man 177;
Isle of Wight 232; Israel 273; Italian 148, 296, 330; Italy
130, 135, 191, 240, 298, 324, 377, 436, 482, 483; iTunes 219;
IVF 137; ivory 157; Ivory Coast 157

Jack Russells 234; Hugh Jackman 196; Michael Jackson 276;
J'Adore perfume 436; James IV of Scotland 497; Japan 54,
103, 113, 118, 153, 300, 404, 409, 443, 451, 495, 496; Japan
pig 290; Japanese 355, 475, 495; Japanese bullfighting 248;
Japanese people 44, 181, 219, 238, 240, 327, 337, 345, 363, 394;
Japanese Self-Defence Forces 503; jars 243, 420; *Jaws* 32, 198;
JD 164; jeans 452; jellyfish 257, 302, 303, 456; jerseys 372;
Jesus Christ 97, 262, 493; jewellers 36; jewellery 49; jewels
36; Jigsaw Puzzle Library 140; *Jimmy Kimmel Live!* 265; Joan
of Arc 44; job-creation schemes 7; jobs 63, 119, 327, 421;
Steve Jobs 67, 351, 467, 482; jockeys 359; Johannesburg 18;
Pope John Paul II 250; Dr Johnson's *Dictionary* 39, 397, 477;
Dwayne 'The Rock' Johnson 273, 274; Lyndon B. Johnson
122, 347; jokes 36; Janis Joplin 444; Josiah 162; jubilees 438;
July 309; jumping 226, 228; June 141; C. G. Jung 409; jungle
486; Jupiter 117, 227; *Jurassic Park* 400; jurors 16, 292

'K' 146; Kafr al-Battikh 195; Theodor Kaluza 320; kangaroo
rats 426; kangaroos 123; Kansas 245; Kansas University
352; Karachi 213; Kashmir 212; Kattenkabinet museum,

menstruation 154; mental alertness 143; menus 328, 381; mercury 275; Mercury 117; Freddie Mercury 276, 481; Angela Merkel 199; Merry Christmas 141; Mesolithic 457; messages 206, 361; messengers 299; metabolism 389; metal 182, 441; metal-workers 441; meteorites 427, 485; methane 227; Metropolitan Police Acts 301; 'Mexican Hat Dance' 68; Mexican yams 27; Mexico 68, 80, 166, 406, 501; Mexico City 130; Stephenie Meyer 143; Miami Beach 252; mice 19, 105, 187, 196, 197; Michigan 421; microbes 15; microphones 21; microplastic 289; microscopic plants 185; Microsoft 52; microwave ovens 437; middle age 87; Middle Ages 93, 188, 312, 335, 388; middle names 458, 472; Middlesbrough 412; midges 449; midlife crises 452; *Mighty Morphin Power Rangers* 233; migraines 309; migration 224; mild 331; military 29; military service 53; milk 58, 89; millennials 4; A. A. Milne 401; mime 38; mimicry 279; mines 285; Minge Lane, Worcester 86; miniaturisation 245; Ministry of Defence 217; minty flavour 208; minute leaf chameleons 304; Misery 431; mispronouncing 'R's 241; mistakes 42, 162, 288, 322; moans 199; mobile phones 49, 59, 60, 211, 384; Moche people 38; mock eggs 121; models 170, 223, 416; Moldova 148, 474; Mole Hill, West Virginia 31; molehills 163; moles 258; Monaco 191; Monday 255; Claude Monet 46; money 20, 134, 149, 202, 382; money-making 382; Mongolian 296; monkeys 147; monks 93; monograms 7; monopolies 390; Monopoly 390; Monte 92; Monte Carlo 191; Montenegro 248; months 156, 179, 323, 359, 360, 375, 499; monuments 424, 430; moods 71; Moon 8, 15, 78, 79, 113, 117, 387, 423; moons 25, 117, 121, 129, 227, 269; moose 196; *Moose Murders* 254; Christopher Morley 122; Morocco 216; morphine 233; Moscow 321; mosquitoes 74, 343; 'Most Wanted' lists 350;

mothers 42, 188, 193, 284, 326, 401, 418, 433, 441; Mother's Day 193; moths 82, 260, 449; motor oil 380; motor vehicles 416; motorcyclists 426; motorways 120; Mount Auburn Cemetery 235; mountaineers 284; mountains 30, 31, 93, 283; mourning 79, 472, 497; mousetraps 314; moustaches 202; mouths 37, 342, 389; movements 226; movie magazines 31; Wolfgang Amadeus Mozart 246; MPs 220, 404, 454; MRSA 486; Mswati III of Swaziland 439; mud 291, 360; muffin-walloper 210; mugs 366; mummification 19, 82; Muppets 481; murder 135, 144, 291; murder mysteries 317; *Murder on the Orient Express* 144; murder scenes 259; murderers 64, 292; murderous 318, 411; murders 411; muscle injuries 152; museums 232; mushrooms 200; music 68, 78, 132, 140, 274, 301; musical accompaniment 229; musical instruments 140, 212; musical notes 440; musing 479; Elon Musk 254; mussels 477; myrrh 374, 459; 'Mysterious Murder in Snowy Cream' 229; mythical heroes 247

nail-biting 471; nails 493; James Naismith 352; naked 487; naked mole rats 259; name-calling 220; name-changing 86, 128, 439, 475, 481, 482; name-recollection 35; Namibia 412; naming 1, 30, 31, 42, 95, 122, 130, 136, 158, 169, 215, 297, 352, 358; Napoleonic Wars 346; NASA 15, 48, 108, 109, 160, 254, 468; national anthem 68; national birds 136; national drinks 335; national mints 52; National Poo Museum 232; NATO 248; Natural History Museum 460; naturalists 477; nature 1; nature reserves 120, 381; naturism 358; naughtiness 160; naval officers 384; navies 503; navigation 380; Nazca people 343; Neanderthals 485; necks 131; needle-swallowing 42; negative connotations 475; negatives 344; neighbours 286; Nelson's Column 445; Nepal 283; nephews 503; Neptune

118; nerve cells 283; nerves 180; Nestlé 488; nests 334; Netflix 114; Netherlands 46, 470; nets 500; Nevadans 464; New Delhi 59; New Guinea 139, 249; New Year's Day 18, 344; New York City 17, 47, 49, 259, 395, 411, 430; New York state 431; New York subway 430; New Zealand 95, 178, 223, 315, 400, 431, 495, 502; newborns 42, 279, 473; news media 274, 441; newspapers 484; Isaac Newton 434; NHS 311; Niagara Falls 235; nicknames 32, 159, 173; night 171, 353, 417, 444; night vision 44, 230; Nile 18, 63; Nintendo 355; nipponium 280; Richard Nixon 162, 347; *NME* 481; 'No More Tours' 132; Noah's Ark 190; nodding along 386; noise 9, 25, 199, 229, 351, 363; noises 289; noisy miners 120; Nomura's jellyfish 302; non-existence 1, 153, 173; nonsense 411; noodle-slurping 363; Norfolk Island, Australia 173; normality 175; Normandy 295; Norse mythology 391; North Korea 117, 394; North Pole 357; North Ronaldsay sheep 91; Northern Ireland 205; Northern Ireland Assembly 362; Northern Lights 329; Norway 355, 456, 457; nose grease 344; nose jobs 24; noses 94, 161, 234, 307, 473; nostalgia 43; nostrils 234; notes 373; noticing 220; Nottingham 417; nouns 2; novels 84, 336, 407; November 309; nuclear facilities 168; nuclear meltdowns 465; nuclear power plants 287; nuclear reactors 167, 168; nuclear strikes 168; nuclear weapons 21, 219; nudist beaches 190; nuisances 126; numbering 116; nurse sharks 281; nurses 478; nursing 189; nutmeg 61; nutrition 414; nuts 323; Michael Nyman 494; NYPD 373

Oakland, California 150; Barack Obama 340; obesity 478; Obi-Two 155; obsessions 3; obsolete 243; obstacle courses 137; obstacles 4; ocean floor 30; ocean gods 25; oceans 380,

photocopying 231; photographic workshops 325; photons 175, 492; photos 20, 94, 96, 99, 244, 344, 345, 480; physicists 494; phytoplankton 185; pianolas 274; pianos 274, 398; Pablo Picasso 172, 232; Piccadilly Line 343; pickpockets 244; picnics 192, 417; Pie Town, New Mexico 95; Piedmontese 130; pie-eating contest 298; pie-maggots 482; pies 48, 95, 297, 298; pig farms 118; pig toilets 114; pigeon racing 16; pigeons 16, 168, 266, 283, 291, 320, 321, 491; Piggy 134; piggy banks 223; piglets 99, 401; pigs 114, 234, 393; Pilates 326; piles 281; pilgrims 128; pillar boxes 275; pillows 237; pills 275; pilots 155, 182; pinball 150; pinching 296; pines 208; pink 258, 434; pinkletink 121; PINs 317; pints 315, 388; pipelines 120; piracy 34, 419; piranhas 102; pisonias 103; Pittsburgh 174; pizza 423; placebo pills 28; placentas 326; plague 139; planets 25, 118, 226, 301; planks 301; plankton 185, 301; planting 6, 161; plants 236, 311, 312, 489, 504; plastic 8, 409; plastic bags 274, 462; plastic bottles 289; plastic ducks 223; plastic garden flamingos 222; plastic straws 9; plastic surgery 24; plastic waste 409; Play-Doh 233; playing cards 373, 492; plays 47, 254; pleasing 335; pleasure 365; Pliny the Elder 154; plumage 333; plumbers 355; Pluto 25, 117, 227, 236; plutonium 251; pneumatic tubes 115; pods 33; poetry 40, 106, 253; poetry competitions 10; pointy 262; poison 444; poison gas 275; poison ivy 471; poisoning 275, 488; poker 150; poker faces 150; Poland 30, 88, 141, 161, 162; polar bears 133; police 30, 32, 96, 112, 161, 173, 174, 178, 205, 285, 329; police interviews 301; police stations 97; Polish 147, 161; political parties 220; polls 424; pollutants 254; *Poltergeist* 25; polyester 430; polyisobutylene 60; Polynesians 268; poo 279, 357; poodles 234, 271; pool 388; pool rooms 388; poor people 149, 176, 202; pop music 132; pop stars 444;

popcorn 386, 428; Pope 89, 90, 135, 142; Popemobile 250;
popes 135; Pope's Head 250; Popeye biceps 152; Popeye butt
152; poppies 346; populations 88; Porgs 156; porn 238, 481;
Portsmouth 170, 171; Portugal 92, 147, 414; Portuguese 146,
147; Poseidon 25; post 76; postal workers 421; postboxes
166, 275; postgraduates 498; posthumous 130; Postman Pat
86; postmen 75, 366; pot 161; pot plants 40; potatoes 36,
81, 160, 161, 233, 379, 423; potions 496; Beatrix Potter 416;
Harry Potter 164; pottos 371; poultry 201; powder 70;
Rickster Powell 187; power cables 331; power stations 287;
power usage 244; practising 7; Prada 403; prairie dogs
351; prairie voles 221; prams 151; prank calls 467; Terry
Pratchett 205; prawn crackers 148; prawn mayonnaise 111;
prawns 147; prayers 384; praying mantises 375; predators
83, 126, 194, 279; predictions 340, 467; pregnancy 470;
prehistoric women 418; Premier League 9; preparation 196,
228, 259; prescriptions 62, 496; present 2; presentations
229; presidential elections 55, 340, 442; presidents 201, 347;
presidents-for-life 263; Elvis Presley 265, 347; pressure 367;
pretence 163, 187, 386, 391, 420; pre-worn 452; prey 279;
prey-tracking 14; price tags 469; pride 39; *Pride and Prejudice*
401; priests 250; primary schools 164; primates 371, 450;
primatologists 371; prime ministers 76, 354, 364; Prime
Minister's Questions 454; prime numbers 23; Primrose Hill
395; Prince 341; printers 204; printing 321; prison sentences
65; prisoners 65, 290, 352, 353; prisoners-of-war 326; prisons
65, 330, 403, 404, 481; private jets 327; private schools 47;
prizes 30, 157; proboscis monkeys 94; procaffeinating 266;
procrastinating 108, 218; Procrastinators' Club of America
108; professionals 28, 474; professors 164, 252; programs
206; Prohibition 62; Prohibition Party 442; projectors 229;

pronunciation 291, 373; Prosecco 141, 474; prosecution 174; prospectors 95; prosthetics 253, 433; protected species 438; protection 181, 328, 461; protein 408, 409; protesters 321; protons 367; Prussian blue 27; psychiatrists 316; *Psycho* 134; psychologists 316; ptarmigan 378; pterodactyls 42; pub names 412; pub quizzes 310; puberty 389; pubic hair 209, 210; public holidays 79, 81, 340; public parks 235; public toilets 114, 368; public transport 466; publishing 106; pubs 75, 145, 165, 249, 250, 415; pucks 207; pudding 298; Puffin Island 156; puffins 70, 156; Chesty Puller 299; pulse 103; Puma 155; pumas 20; pumpkin toadlets 194; punchball 291; punches 291; punch-ups 277; punctuality 157; punctuation 353; punishments 209, 216; Punjab 212; punting 138; puppies 244; purgatory 65; Purgatory Correctional Facility 65; purple 341; purpose 365; purses 244; Pyrenees 446; Pythagoras 64; pythons 428, 473

'Q' 146; Qatar 496; *QE2* 270; Qin dynasty 54; Qin Shi Huang 275; Qing dynasty 237; Quaker Oats 469; Quakers 469; qualification 200; quantum physics 1; Quebec 32; Queen 293; queens 460; Queen's Speech 7; questions 364; quetzal birds 491; queues 270; James Quin 291; quinine 74, 329; QuizTeam Aguilera 310

rabbits 20, 179, 307; Sergei Rachmaninov 398; radiation 15; radio 21, 160; radio stations 159, 160; radioactivity 287; RAF 87; raffles 157; rain 71, 320, 474; rainforest 486; Rameses III 63; Range Rovers 333; rank 88, 131; ransom note effect 464; rappers 8; raptors in flight 183; raspberry-blowing 267; Rasputin 432; rat farms 395; rationing 98; rats 6, 99, 369, 395, 430; rattles 156; Ravenmaster 446; ravens 446; ravioli

269; reading 2, 65, 161, 284, 353, 407, 480; Ronald Reagan
21, 359; rear-view mirrors 273; rebranding 52; recalls 230;
recipes 111, 238; recognition 127, 217, 283, 320, 435, 475;
record-burning 21; recording 276; recruitment 252; rectum
197; recycling 60, 401; recycling bins 60; red 27, 28, 36; red
flags 361; Red Lion 249; red pandas 120, 450; red sea urchins
402; red-sided garter snakes 187; Redundant Acronym
Syndrome 317; Reed College 168; re-enactments 91; re-
entry 442; referees 29, 73, 207; referendums 454; reflections
333; Reformation 250; refreshment rooms 325; refusals 41,
50, 64, 161, 499; refuse workers 422; reggae 132; Regina,
California 16; registration 300; regurgitating 491; reindeer
176; rejected names 280; relatedness 259; relatives 339;
relaxed 270; religious belief 448; religious ceremonies 448;
religious cults 501; Rembrandt 46, 232; remedies 61, 279;
Remember 128; remembrance 149; reminders 273; removal
2, 107, 209, 262; renaming 31; renovation 255; renting 92,
250, 257; repatriation 450; replicas 22, 184, 445; reporters
364; repulsion 179; rescues 246; research 252; researchers
196, 211, 219, 321, 354, 430; resemblances 162; the reservoir
482; Resolve 128; restaurants 32, 112, 353; rests 448; retail
industry 29; retirement age 214, 238; retrials 292; reusable
toilet paper 98; Reuters 321; 'Reverse Canterbury Pleasure'
206; rewards 312; Rheinsberg 167; Rhinoceros Party 442;
rhinos 423; rhubarb 422; rhymes 309; ribbons 131; Christina
Ricci 310; rice 345; rich people 97, 202, 232, 487; Sally Ride
254; 'Ride of the Valkyries' 68; rifles 462; rigid 193; ringing
206, 224, 363; rings 255; rings of Saturn 121, 225; Rio 129;
riot squads 418; riots 47, 417; ripeness 337; risk 255; Rita
169; Ritalin 169; Ritz-Carlton hotel, Riyadh 403; rivals 333,
449; rivers 126; road deaths 437; road markings 289; road

quality 116; road salt 121; roadside inns 116; roasts 154, 349; robins 58, 389; Tom Robinson 444; robot bees 468; robotic noses 94; robots 94, 133, 251, 294, 354; Robutt 133; Rock, Paper, Scissors 371; rocks 225, 385, 388; roles 196; roller skates 299; roller skis 299; *Rolling Stone* 445; Rolls-Royce Phantom 70; Romania 119; Rome 112, 416; *Ronald Reagan* 302; Wilhelm Röntgen 231; roofs 83, 123, 320; rooms 191; Franklin D. Roosevelt 356, 499; Theodore Roosevelt 145, 162; roosters 292, 428; Rosetta Stone 65; rotating 332; rottenness 120, 160; Rottweilers 234; roundabouts 393; roundness 273; rowing 418, 419; J. K. Rowling 331; rows 126; Royal Bastards Society 497; royal estates 9; royal family 128, 465; Royal Mint 243; Royal Navy 465, 503; Royal Society for the Protection of Birds 399; royalty 63; rubber bands 207; rubber ducks 371; rubbers 390; rubbish 78; rubbish dumps 78; rubies 36; Amber Rudd 400; rude names 159; rugby 345; rules 17, 220, 270; rulings 26, 81; running 107, 264, 414; running over 73; rushing 475; Russia 21, 212, 214, 222, 244, 309, 327, 418, 424, 465; Russian 13, 88, 424; Russian intelligence service 53; Rwanda 201

'S' 308; sacred combat 38; sadness 383, 505; safety mascots 468; Sahara desert 264, 427; sailors 216; sails 216; St Andrews 271; St Bernard 101; St David's 477; St Paul's, Papanui 224; saints 44; sales 60, 111; salmonella 350; salt 476; salt spoons 357; salt and vinegar 269; salt-spreading trucks 78; SAM 502; Sami people 196; Samsung 457; samurai 503; San Francisco 10, 113, 300; San Marino 416; sand 129, 176, 205, 252; sandcastles 129; Colonel Sanders 305; Tennys Sandgren 169; sandwiches 111, 329; Santa Claus 160; Santo Tomás, Peru 277; Sardinia 129; Saturn 117, 121,

129, 225, 269; Saudi Arabia 94, 386, 414, 487; saunas 99; Sausage Swiper 160; sausages 50, 51, 337; Facundo Sava 413; Savannah 19; scales 225; Scandinavia 414; scaring off 194; scarlet 434; Harrison Schmitt 442; school mottos 419; school projects 214; schoolchildren 46, 297; schools 300, 442, 443; Arnold Schwarzenegger 367; scientific papers 317, 367; scientific studies 418; scientists 56, 101, 137, 140, 157, 211, 216, 259, 303, 421, 494; scores 494; scorpion-milking machines 216; Scotland 5, 72, 78, 93, 181, 335, 449, 497; Scots 71, 196, 335; Sir Walter Scott 336; Scottish 455; scratches 371; screaming women 490; screens 211; scuba diving 447; sculptors 223; sculptures 307; sea 251, 289, 409, 505; sea ice 456; sea lions 318; sea slugs 138; sea urchins 91, 175, 261, 385, 453; seabed 281; seagulls 112; seahorses 290; searching 3, 178, 372; seasons 372; seats 182, 333; Seattle 157; Seattle-Tacoma airport 281; seaweed 91; Second World War 48, 53, 83, 98, 99, 185, 275, 362, 376, 393; secondary education 499; second-hand bookshops 84; second-hand shops 253; secrecy 12, 163; secret messages 69; secret passageways 135; secret pubs 408; security guards 404; security scanners 197; seedpods 204; seeds 346, 506; seeing 175, 375; seeing through 230, 231; Seine 16, 100; self-defence 396; selfies 94; self-service tills 53; selling 50, 95, 100, 105, 126, 230, 263, 304, 366; semen 137; semihemidemisemiquavers 440; senior citizens 95; sentences 143; sequins 482; Serbia 244; Serbian 244; *Sgt. Pepper* 112; serpents 477; sesame seeds 406; *Sesame Street* 410; settees 434; settlements 362; sewers 459; sewing kits 80; sex 22, 105, 162, 174, 186, 187, 211, 247, 306, 322, 342, 430, 449; sex workers 174; sexual urges 323; sexy primes 23; Seychelles 146; shades 374; shag 424; William Shakespeare 297; shaking 180, 319; Shall 122; shaming 38;

shampoo 136; shareholders 184, 256; sharing 459; shark attacks 303; sharks 32, 124, 183, 198; William Shatner 368; shaving 175, 257; shaving foam 257; sheep 72, 123, 137, 239, 338, 339, 366, 367, 410; sheep fighting 276; sheepdogs 181; sheets 149; Mary Shelley 253, 284; shells 484; shelves 138; Shenzi 280; shin pads 372; shipping containers 361; shipping lanes 392; ships 356, 391; shirts 412; shiver 183; shoes 128, 261, 262, 340; shooting 105, 133, 172, 292, 351, 416; shooting down 356; shop assistants 119; shopping 60; shopping bags 409; shops 126; shoreline 409; short stories 10; short-sightedness 364; shoulder-shrugging 14; shoulder-tapping 14; shouting 83, 85, 347; shouting bombs 83; shower curtains 487; showers 388; shrews 127; shrubs 250; Siberia 490; Sichuan 42; sick 478; Sierra Leone 273; Sierra Negra, Battle of the 24; sight 69, 249; sign language 101; signalling 440; signature 475; signs 191, 214, 307; silencing 255; silent films 229; Silicon Valley 389; Silly Walks 241; silverware 39; Queen Silvia of Sweden 284; *The Simpsons* 97, 340; simulations 133; Sindh 212; Singapore 140, 354, 496; singing 383, 449; singles 132, 191; sinkings 430; sins 337; sitting 133, 424; sitting-volleyball 425; six 338; skating 277; skeletons 231, 232; sketching 14; ski lifts 339; skiing 213, 299; skin 193, 385; skipping 387; skulls 171, 238; skunk cabbages 179; sky 96, 436; skyaking 447; skydiving 441, 447; skyscrapers 402; slackers 210; slang 75, 130, 147, 210, 285, 305, 330, 382; slapstick 324; sled runners 213; sleep 57, 71, 95, 126, 267, 281, 338, 400, 473; *Sleepless in Seattle* 281; sleeves 216, 293; sliced bread 111; slicing open 244; Slinkys 501; slits 234; slogans 442; sloths 362, 396, 456; slouching 325; Slovakia 68; Slovenia 470; slugs 459; small change 119; smartphones 48, 59, 467; smell 74, 194, 211, 233, 272, 283, 371, 384, 407, 483;

290, 361; strippers 149; stripping 106; Strong Drinks
Museum 148; Mr Stubley 169; students 17, 498; studios 276;
stuffing 82; stunts 246, 324; sub-machine guns 351;
submarine 251; submarines 79; subterranean 251; sucking
319; suffrage 177; suffragettes 76; sugar 181, 318, 319; suicide
444; suing 305; summer 127, 237, 372; summits 30; sumo
475, 476; Sun 69, 118, 237; Sun Tan Drews 271; sunscreen
103, 272; Suomi 458; Super Bowl 286; Super Mario 226, 355;
superb bird-of-paradise 57; superionic ice 93; supermarkets
50, 138, 256; supersonic flypasts 22; suppliers 256; surgeons
24; surnames 77, 128, 222, 295; surrenders 144; surveys 107,
108; survival 369, 375, 378, 402, 426; sushi 238, 345; suspicion
161; swabbing 211; Swahili 280; swallowing 14, 491; swans
on land 183; swarms 468; swastikas 145; swatches 383; swear
words 29; sweat 286, 405; Roger Sweatinbed 286; Sweden 4,
66, 171, 203, 228, 287, 313, 361, 394, 465; Swedish 295, 296,
438; sweets 413; swimming 16, 17, 34, 58, 126, 320, 331, 375,
456; swimming caps 240; swimming costumes 17; swimming
pools 17, 240; SWIPERS 29; Swiss Air Force 455; Swiss
Army 439, 440; Switzerland 292, 347, 375, 439, 454, 459;
swordfish 14; swords 454; symbols 346; symphonies 172,
440; symptom-relief 349; synchronising 114, 176; Syria 490

table tennis 28; tackles 372; taglines 232; Tahitian 505;
tails 57, 123, 395, 473; tail-shedding 279; Taiwan 78, 321;
Taj Mahal 319; taking off 491; talk radio 20; talking about
self 296; talking stamps 166; tampons 254; Tancítaro,
Mexico 173; tanks 482; tanning salons 271; tapestries 80;
tarantulas 122; tarmac 299; tartan 335; tasers 29, 367;
tasks 197; Tasmania 250; taste 338, 450; taste buds 208,
306; Tate 170; tattoos 239, 240, 433; taupe 258; taverns 75;

433; umbilical cords 58; umbrellas 70, 230; UN 146, 214; uncensored 317; unconsciousness 211, 247; undercover police 112, 285; undergraduates 168; underground streets 474; underpants 43, 178, 242, 417; understanding 490; undertakers 87; underwater pipelines 98; undrinkable 117; unfinished works 205; unfitness 302; uniforms 75, 372; uniqueness 204; universe 2, 492, 506; University of Hawaii 494; University of Illinois 105; University of Miami 252; unmarried 313; unprofessional 364; upper classes 39; upside down 314; upside-down catfish 375; uranium 251; Uranus 117, 118; Uranus Road 159; Pope Urban VIII 135; urban slang 51; urges 106, 296, 365; urinating 276; urine 27, 42, 57, 105, 315; US 21, 55, 62, 88, 91, 111, 119, 167, 201, 219, 241, 252, 267, 287, 319, 328, 352, 393, 404, 455, 487; US Centers for Disease Control and Prevention 350; US Air Force 83, 356; US Army 98; US civil defence 168; US Congress 410, 448; US Flag Code 214; US government 359, 396, 502; US military 43, 98, 131, 299, 438; US National Parks 235; US Navy 356, 503; US Postal Service 480; US Postmaster General 55; US presidency 55, 137, 340, 473; US Senate 442; US states 190, 315; US Supreme Court 81; US Transportation Security Administration 445; US TV 199; USA 502; useless information 270; Useless Islands 431; USSR 153; Utah 65, 82; uteruses 186; Uzi 351

Valium 233; valuable plants 330; Vincent van Gogh 46, 381; vancomycin 486; Vanuatu 161; varieties 219, 323; Vatican 89, 135, 336, 501; vats 315; veganism 26, 271; vegetables 81; vegetarianism 26, 236; vending machines 10, 495; Venezuela 427; Venice 170; venom 215, 216; Venus 109, 117, 334; Venus flytraps 334; Viagra 27, 43; Vicks VapoRub 496; victims 291;

Las Vegas 191; welcomes 212; H. G. Wells 11; Welsh 339, 379; Welsh mythology 247, 391; Wembley stadium 474; 'Big Bill' Werbeniuk 388; werewhales 196; werewolves 196; West Berlin 309; West End 47; western Europe 220; Western Front 179; westwards 487; wet 320; JD Wetherspoon 164; Wettin 128; whale meatballs 443; whales 198, 385; wheels 49; *Where in the World Is Osama bin Laden?* 67; whippets 360; whistles 207; whistling 228, 446; white 309, 434; 'White Christmas' 229; white coats 152; White House 55, 246, 381; *Who's Who* 84; Whynot, North Carolina 158; wickerwork 182; Wigan 48, 298; wild parrots 259; Oscar Wilde 353, 480; wildfires 279; Wildlife Trust 381; Will 122; Willey Lane 159; Prince William 413; William of Prussia 161; Venus Williams 387; Gavin Williamson 122; Thomas Wilmot 149; Wimbledon 169, 387, 461; wind 106, 477; wind turbines 477; windfalls 385; windows 18, 260, 302, 365, 492; Windows 95 67; Windsor Castle 128, 165; wine 221, 498; wine cellars 246, 474; wine glasses 142; wingspans 33, 182; winning 290, 390; winnings 165; winter 127, 237; Winter Olympics 213, 299; Wisconsin 32; wistfulness 84; witty ripostes 35; wives 75, 169, 222, 473; *The Wizard of Oz* 467; wobbly furniture 420; wolf whistles 181; Wolverine 196; wolves 181, 196, 293, 294, 303, 395; wombs 37, 186, 238; Wonder Woman 13; wood 493, 494; wood frogs 193; woodchucks 59; wood-mice 419; woodpeckers 405; wool 430; woolly mammoths 157, 264; wordiness 218; words 3, 163, 317, 320; workers 38, 54, 197, 254, 329, 418, 421, 478; working 420; World Bollard Association 272; world championship 324; World Cups 29, 195, 202, 426; World Mobile Phone Throwing Championships 212; World Pie Eating Championship 48; world records 188, 314, 397, 401; World Snooker Championship 352; World